Five Plays, Set 2:

There Are Crimes And Crimes; Miss Julia; The Stronger; Creditors; Pariah

by

August Strindberg

D1504842

The Echo Library 2006

Published by

The Echo Library

Echo Library
131 High St.
Teddington
Middlesex TW11 8HH

www.echo-library.com

Please report serious faults in the text to complaints@echo-library.com

ISBN 1-40680-790-7

CONTENTS

THERE ARE CRIMES AND CRIMES

INTRODUCTION

STRINDBERG was fifty years old when he wrote "There Are Crimes and Crimes." In the same year, 1899, he produced three of his finest historical dramas: "The Saga of the Folkungs," "Gustavus Vasa," and "Eric XIV." Just before, he had finished "Advent," which he described as "A Mystery," and which was published together with "There Are Crimes and Crimes" under the common title of "In a Higher Court." Back of these dramas lay his strange confessional works, "Inferno" and "Legends," and the first two parts of his autobiographical dream-play, "Toward Damascus"—all of which were finished between May, 1897, and some time in the latter part of 1898. And back of these again lay that period of mental crisis, when, at Paris, in 1895 and 1896, he strove to make gold by the transmutation of baser metals, while at the same time his spirit was travelling through all the seven hells in its search for the heaven promised by the great mystics of the past.

"There Are Crimes and Crimes" may, in fact, be regarded as his first definite step beyond that crisis, of which the preceding works were at once the record and closing chord. When, in 1909, he issued "The Author," being a long withheld fourth part of his first autobiographical series, "The Bondwoman's Son," he prefixed to it an analytical summary of the entire body of his work. Opposite the works from 1897-8 appears in this summary the following passage: "The great crisis at the age of fifty; revolutions in the life of the soul, desert wanderings, Swedenborgian Heavens and Hells." But concerning "There Are Crimes and Crimes" and the three historical dramas from the same year he writes triumphantly: "Light after darkness; new productivity, with recovered Faith, Hope and Love—and with full, rock-firm Certitude."

In its German version the play is named "Rausch," or "Intoxication," which indicates the part played by the champagne in the plunge of *Maurice* from the pinnacles of success to the depths of misfortune. Strindberg has more and more come to see that a moderation verging closely on asceticism is wise for most men and essential to the man of genius who wants to fulfil his divine mission. And he does not scorn to press home even this comparatively humble lesson with the naive directness and fiery zeal which form such conspicuous features of all his work.

But in the title which bound it to "Advent" at their joint publication we have a better clue to what the author himself undoubtedly regards as the most important element of his work—its religious tendency. The "higher court," in which are tried the crimes of *Maurice*, *Adolphe*, and *Henriette*, is, of course, the highest one that man can imagine. And the crimes of which they have all become guilty are those which, as *Adolphe* remarks, "are not mentioned in the criminal code"—in a word, crimes against the spirit, against the impalpable power that moves us, against God. The play, seen in this light, pictures a deep-reaching spiritual change, leading us step by step from the soul adrift on the waters of life to the state where it is definitely oriented and impelled.

There are two distinct currents discernible in this dramatic revelation of progress from spiritual chaos to spiritual order— for to order the play must be said to lead, and progress is implied in its onward movement, if there be anything at all in our growing modern conviction that *any* vital faith is better than none at all. One of the currents in question refers to the means rather than the end, to the road rather than the goal. It brings us back to those uncanny soul-adventures by which Strindberg himself won his way to the "full, rock-firm Certitude" of which the play in its entirety is the first tangible expression. The elements entering into this current are not only mystical, but occult. They are derived in part from Swedenborg, and in part from that picturesque French dreamer who signs himself "Sar Péladan"; but mostly they have sprung out of Strindberg's own experiences in moments of abnormal tension.

What happened, or seemed to happen, to himself at Paris in 1895, and what he later described with such bewildering exactitude in his "Inferno" and "Legends," all this is here presented in dramatic form, but a little toned down, both to suit the needs of the stage and the calmer mood of the author. Coincidence is law. It is the finger-point of Providence, the signal to man that he must beware. Mystery is the gospel: the secret knitting of man to man, of fact to fact, deep beneath the surface of visible and audible existence. Few writers could take us into such a realm of probable impossibilities and possible improbabilities without losing all claim to serious consideration. If Strindberg has thus ventured to our gain and no loss of his own, his success can be explained only by the presence in the play of that second, parallel current of thought and feeling.

This deeper current is as simple as the one nearer the surface is fantastic. It is the manifestation of that "rock-firm Certitude" to which I have already referred. And nothing will bring us nearer to it than Strindberg's own confession of faith, given in his "Speeches to the Swedish Nation" two years ago. In that pamphlet there is a chapter headed "Religion," in which occurs this passage: "Since 1896 I have been calling myself a Christian. I am not a Catholic, and have never been, but during a stay of seven years in Catholic countries and among Catholic relatives, I discovered that the difference between Catholic and Protestant tenets is either none at all, or else wholly superficial, and that the division which once occurred was merely political or else concerned with theological problems not fundamentally germane to the religion itself. A registered Protestant I am and will remain, but I can hardly be called orthodox or evangelistic, but come nearest to being a Swedenborgian. I use my Bible Christianity internally and privately to tame my somewhat decivilized nature— decivilised by that veterinary philosophy and animal science (Darwinism) in which, as student at the university, I was reared. And I assure my fellow-beings that they have no right to complain because, according to my ability, I practise the Christian teachings. For only through religion, or the hope of something better, and the recognition of the innermost meaning of life as that of an ordeal, a school, or perhaps a penitentiary, will it be possible to bear the burden of life with sufficient resignation."

Here, as elsewhere, it is made patent that Strindberg's religiosity always, on closer analysis, reduces itself to morality. At bottom he is first and last, and has always been, a moralist—a man passionately craving to know what is RIGHT and to do it. During the middle, naturalistic period of his creative career, this fundamental tendency was in part obscured, and he engaged in the game of intellectual curiosity known as "truth for truth's own sake." One of the chief marks of his final and mystical period is his greater courage to "be himself" in this respect—and this means necessarily a return, or an advance, to a position which the late William James undoubtedly would have acknowledged as "pragmatic." To combat the assertion of over-developed individualism that we are ends in ourselves, that we have certain inalienable personal "rights" to pleasure and happiness merely because we happen to appear here in human shape, this is one of Strindberg's most ardent aims in all his later works.

As to the higher and more inclusive object to which our lives must be held subservient, he is not dogmatic. It may be another life. He calls it God. And the code of service he finds in the tenets of all the Christian churches, but principally in the Commandments. The plain and primitive virtues, the faith that implies little more than square dealing between man and man—these figure foremost in Strindberg's ideals. In an age of supreme self-seeking like ours, such an outlook would seem to have small chance of popularity, but that it embodies just what the time most needs is, perhaps, made evident by the reception which the public almost invariably grants "There Are Crimes and Crimes" when it is staged.

With all its apparent disregard of what is commonly called realism, and with its occasional, but quite unblushing, use of methods generally held superseded—such as the casual introduction of characters at whatever moment they happen to be needed on the stage—it has, from the start, been among the most frequently played and most enthusiastically received of Strindberg's later dramas. At Stockholm it was first taken up by the Royal Dramatic Theatre, and was later seen on the tiny stage of the Intimate Theatre, then devoted exclusively to Strindberg's works. It was one of the earliest plays staged by Reinhardt while he was still experimenting with his Little Theatre at Berlin, and it has also been given in numerous German cities, as well as in Vienna.

Concerning my own version of the play I wish to add a word of explanation. Strindberg has laid the scene in Paris. Not only the scenery, but the people and the circumstances are French. Yet he has made no attempt whatever to make the dialogue reflect French manners of speaking or ways of thinking. As he has given it to us, the play is French only in its most superficial aspect, in its setting—and this setting he has chosen simply because he needed a certain machinery offered him by the Catholic, but not by the Protestant, churches. The rest of the play is purely human in its note and wholly universal in its spirit. For this reason I have retained the French names and titles, but have otherwise striven to bring everything as close as possible to our own modes of expression. Should apparent incongruities result from this manner of treatment, I think they will disappear if only the reader will try to remember that the characters of the play move in an existence cunningly woven by the author out of scraps of ephemeral reality in order that he may show us the mirage of a more enduring one.

THERE ARE CRIMES AND CRIMES
A COMEDY
1899

CHARACTERS

> MAURICE, a playwright
> JEANNE, his mistress
> MARION, their daughter, five years old
> ADOLPHE, a painter
> HENRIETTE, his mistress
> EMILE, a workman, brother of Jeanne
> MADAME CATHERINE
> THE ABBÉ
> A WATCHMAN
> A HEAD WAITER
> A COMMISSAIRE
> TWO DETECTIVES
> A WAITER
> A GUARD
> SERVANT GIRL

(All the scenes are laid in Paris)

ACT I
FIRST SCENE

(THE upper avenue of cypresses in the Montparnasse Cemetery at Paris. The background shows mortuary chapels, stone crosses on which are inscribed "O Crux! Ave Spes Unica!" and the ruins of a wind-mill covered with ivy.)

(A well-dressed woman in widow's weeds is kneeling and muttering prayers in front of a grave decorated with flowers.)

(JEANNE is walking back and forth as if expecting somebody.)

(MARION is playing with some withered flowers picked from a rubbish heap on the ground.)

(The ABBÉ is reading his breviary while walking along the further end of the avenue.)

WATCHMAN. [Enters and goes up to JEANNE] Look here, this is no playground.

JEANNE. [Submissively] I am only waiting for somebody who'll soon be here—

WATCHMAN. All right, but you're not allowed to pick any flowers.

JEANNE. [To MARION] Drop the flowers, dear.

ABBÉ. [Comes forward and is saluted by the WATCHMAN] Can't the child play with the flowers that have been thrown away?

WATCHMAN. The regulations don't permit anybody to touch even the flowers that have been thrown away, because it's believed they may spread infection—which I don't know if it's true.

ABBÉ. [To MARION] In that case we have to obey, of course. What's your name, my little girl?

MARION. My name is Marion.

ABBÉ. And who is your father?

(MARION begins to bite one of her fingers and does not answer.)

ABBÉ. Pardon my question, madame. I had no intention—I was just talking to keep the little one quiet.

(The WATCHMAN has gone out.)

JEANNE. I understood it, Reverend Father, and I wish you would say something to quiet me also. I feel very much disturbed after having waited here two hours.

ABBÉ. Two hours—for him! How these human beings torture each other! O Crux! Ave spes unica!

JEANNE. What do they mean, those words you read all around here?

ABBÉ. They mean: O cross, our only hope!

JEANNE. Is it the only one?

ABBÉ. The only certain one.

JEANNE. I shall soon believe that you are right, Father.

ABBÉ. May I ask why?

JEANNE. You have already guessed it. When he lets the woman and the child wait two hours in a cemetery, then the end is not far off.

ABBÉ. And when he has left you, what then?

JEANNE. Then we have to go into the river.

ABBÉ. Oh, no, no!

JEANNE. Yes, yes!

MARION. Mamma, I want to go home, for I am hungry.

JEANNE. Just a little longer, dear, and we'll go home.

ABBÉ. Woe unto those who call evil good and good evil.

JEANNE. What is that woman doing at the grave over there?

ABBÉ. She seems to be talking to the dead.

JEANNE. But you cannot do that?

ABBÉ. She seems to know how.

JEANNE. This would mean that the end of life is not the end of our misery?

ABBÉ. And you don't know it?

JEANNE. Where can I find out?

ABBÉ. Hm! The next time you feel as if you wanted to learn about this well-known matter, you can look me up in Our Lady's Chapel at the Church of St. Germain—Here comes the one you are waiting for, I guess.

JEANNE. [Embarrassed] No, he is not the one, but I know him.

ABBÉ. [To MARION] Good-bye, little Marion! May God take care of you! [Kisses the child and goes out] At St. Germain des Prés.

EMILE. [Enters] Good morning, sister. What are you doing here?

JEANNE. I am waiting for Maurice.

EMILE. Then I guess you'll have a lot of waiting to do, for I saw him on the boulevard an hour ago, taking breakfast with some friends. [Kissing the child] Good morning, Marion.

JEANNE. Ladies also?

EMILE. Of course. But that doesn't mean anything. He writes plays, and his latest one has its first performance tonight. I suppose he had with him some of the actresses.

JEANNE. Did he recognise you?

EMILE. No, he doesn't know who I am, and it is just as well. I know my place as a workman, and I don't care for any condescension from those that are above me.

JEANNE. But if he leaves us without anything to live on?

EMILE. Well, you see, when it gets that far, then I suppose I shall have to introduce myself. But you don't expect anything of the kind, do you—seeing that he is fond of you and very much attached to the child?

JEANNE. I don't know, but I have a feeling that something dreadful is in store for me.

EMILE. Has he promised to marry you?

JEANNE. No, not promised exactly, but he has held out hopes.

EMILE. Hopes, yes! Do you remember my words at the start: don't hope for anything, for those above us don't marry downward.

JEANNE. But such things have happened.

EMILE. Yes, they have happened. But, would you feel at home in his world? I can't believe it, for you wouldn't even understand what they were talking of. Now and then I take my meals where he is eating—out in the kitchen is my place, of course—and I don't make out a word of what they say.

JEANNE. So you take your meals at that place?

EMILE. Yes, in the kitchen.

JEANNE. And think of it, he has never asked me to come with him.

EMILE. Well, that's rather to his credit, and it shows he has some respect for the mother of his child. The women over there are a queer lot.

JEANNE. Is that so?

EMILE. But Maurice never pays any attention to the women. There is something *square* about that fellow.

JEANNE. That's what I feel about him, too, but as soon as there is a woman in it, a man isn't himself any longer.

EMILE. [Smiling] You don't tell me! But listen: are you hard up for money?

JEANNE. No, nothing of that kind.

EMILE. Well, then the worst hasn't come yet—Look! Over there! There he comes. And I'll leave you. Good-bye, little girl.

JEANNE. Is he coming? Yes, that's him.

EMILE. Don't make him mad now—with your jealousy, Jeanne! [Goes out.]

JEANNE. No, I won't.

(MAURICE enters.)

MARION. [Runs up to him and is lifted up into his arms] Papa, papa!

MAURICE. My little girl! [Greets JEANNE] Can you forgive me, Jeanne, that I have kept you waiting so long?

JEANNE. Of course I can.

MAURICE. But say it in such a way that I can hear that you are forgiving me.

JEANNE. Come here and let me whisper it to you.

(MAURICE goes up close to her.)

(JEANNE kisses him on the cheek.)

MAURICE. I didn't hear.

(JEANNE kisses him on the mouth.)

MAURICE. Now I heard! Well—you know, I suppose that this is the day that will settle my fate? My play is on for tonight, and there is every chance that it will succeed—or fail.

JEANNE. I'll make sure of success by praying for you.

MAURICE. Thank you. If it doesn't help, it can at least do no harm—Look over there, down there in the valley, where the haze is thickest: there lies Paris. Today Paris doesn't know who Maurice is, but it is going to know within twenty-four hours. The haze, which has kept me obscured for thirty years, will vanish before my breath, and I shall become visible, I shall assume definite shape and begin to be somebody. My enemies—which means all who would like to do what I have done—will be writhing in pains that shall be my pleasures, for they will be suffering all that I have suffered.

JEANNE. Don't talk that way, don't!

MAURICE. But that's the way it is.

JEANNE. Yes, but don't speak of it—And then?

MAURICE. Then we are on firm ground, and then you and Marion will bear the name I have made famous.

JEANNE. You love me then?

MAURICE. I love both of you, equally much, or perhaps Marion a little more.

JEANNE. I am glad of it, for you can grow tired of me, but not of her.

MAURICE. Have you no confidence in my feelings toward you?

JEANNE. I don't know, but I am afraid of something, afraid of something terrible—

MAURICE. You are tired out and depressed by your long wait, which once more I ask you to forgive. What have you to be afraid of?

JEANNE. The unexpected: that which you may foresee without having any particular reason to do so.

MAURICE. But I foresee only success, and I have particular reasons for doing so: the keen instincts of the management and their knowledge of the public, not to speak of their personal acquaintance with the critics. So now you must be in good spirits—

JEANNE. I can't, I can't! Do you know, there was an Abbé here a while ago, who talked so beautifully to us. My faith—which you haven't destroyed, but just covered up, as when you put chalk on a window to clean it—I couldn't lay hold on it for that reason, but this old man just passed his hand over the chalk, and the light came through, and it was possible again to see that the people within were at home—To-night I will pray for you at St. Germain.

MAURICE. Now I am getting scared.

JEANNE. Fear of God is the beginning of wisdom.

MAURICE. God? What is that? Who is he?

JEANNE. It was he who gave joy to your youth and strength to your manhood. And it is he who will carry us through the terrors that lie ahead of us.

MAURICE. What is lying ahead of us? What do you know? Where have you learned of this? This thing that I don't know?

JEANNE. I can't tell. I have dreamt nothing, seen nothing, heard nothing. But during these two dreadful hours I have experienced such an infinity of pain that I am ready for the worst.

MARION. Now I want to go home, mamma, for I am hungry.

MAURICE. Yes, you'll go home now, my little darling. [Takes her into his arms.]

MARION. [Shrinking] Oh, you hurt me, papa!

JEANNE. Yes, we must get home for dinner. Good-bye then, Maurice. And good luck to you!

MAURICE. [To MARION] How did I hurt you? Doesn't my little girl know that I always want to be nice to her?

MARION. If you are nice, you'll come home with us.

MAURICE. [To JEANNE] When I hear the child talk like that, you know, I feel as if I ought to do what she says. But then reason and duty protest—Good-bye, my dear little girl! [He kisses the child, who puts her arms around his neck.]

JEANNE. When do we meet again?

MAURICE. We'll meet tomorrow, dear. And then we'll never part again.

JEANNE. [Embraces him] Never, never to part again! [She makes the sign of the cross on his forehead] May God protect you!

MAURICE. [Moved against his own will] My dear, beloved Jeanne!

(JEANNE and MARION go toward the right; MAURICE toward the left. Both turn around simultaneously and throw kisses at each other.)

MAURICE. [Comes back] Jeanne, I am ashamed of myself. I am always forgetting you, and you are the last one to remind me of it. Here are the tickets for tonight.

JEANNE. Thank you, dear, but—you have to take up your post of duty alone, and so I have to take up mine—with Marion.

MAURICE. Your wisdom is as great as the goodness of your heart. Yes, I am sure no other woman would have sacrificed a pleasure to serve her husband—I must have my hands free tonight, and there is no place for women and children on the battle-field—and this you understood!

JEANNE. Don't think too highly of a poor woman like myself, and then you'll have no illusions to lose. And now you'll see that I can be as forgetful as you—I have bought you a tie and a pair of gloves which I thought you might wear for my sake on your day of honour.

MAURICE. [Kissing her hand] Thank you, dear.

JEANNE. And then, Maurice, don't forget to have your hair fixed, as you do all the time. I want you to be good-looking, so that others will like you too.

MAURICE. There is no jealousy in *you*!

JEANNE. Don't mention that word, for evil thoughts spring from it.

MAURICE. Just now I feel as if I could give up this evening's victory—for I am going to win—

JEANNE. Hush, hush!

MAURICE. And go home with you instead.

JEANNE. But you mustn't do that! Go now: your destiny is waiting for you.

MAURICE. Good-bye then! And may that happen which must happen! [Goes out.]

JEANNE. [Alone with MARION] O Crux! Ave spes unica!

(Curtain.)

SECOND SCENE

(THE Crêmerie. On the right stands a buffet, on which are placed an aquarium with goldfish and dishes containing vegetables, fruit, preserves, etc. In the background is a door leading to the kitchen, where workmen are taking their meals. At the other end of the kitchen can be seen a door leading out to a garden. On the left, in the background, stands a counter on a raised platform, and back of it are shelves containing all sorts of bottles. On the right, a long table with a marble top is placed along the wall, and another table is placed parallel to the first further out on the floor. Straw-bottomed chairs stand around the tables. The walls are covered with oil-paintings.)

(MME. CATHERINE is sitting at the counter.)

(MAURICE stands leaning against it. He has his hat on and is smoking a cigarette.)

MME. CATHERINE. So it's tonight the great event comes off, Monsieur Maurice?

MAURICE. Yes, tonight.

MME. CATHERINE. Do you feel upset?

MAURICE. Cool as a cucumber.

MME. CATHERINE. Well, I wish you luck anyhow, and you have deserved it, Monsieur Maurice, after having had to fight against such difficulties as yours.

MAURICE. Thank you, Madame Catherine. You have been very kind to me, and without your help I should probably have been down and out by this time.

MME. CATHERINE. Don't let us talk of that now. I help along where I see hard work and the right kind of will, but I don't want to be exploited—Can we trust you to come back here after the play and let us drink a glass with you?

MAURICE. Yes, you can—of course, you can, as I have already promised you.

(HENRIETTE enters from the right.)

(MAURICE turns around, raises his hat, and stares at HENRIETTE, who looks him over carefully.)

HENRIETTE. Monsieur Adolphe is not here yet?

MME. CATHERINE. No, madame. But he'll soon be here now. Won't you sit down?

HENRIETTE. No, thank you, I'll rather wait for him outside. [Goes out.]

MAURICE. Who—was—that?

MME. CATHERINE. Why, that's Monsieur Adolphe's friend.

MAURICE. Was—that—her?

MME. CATHERINE. Have you never seen her before?

MAURICE. No, he has been hiding her from me, just as if he was afraid I might take her away from him.

MME. CATHERINE. Ha-ha!—Well, how did you think she looked?

MAURICE. How she looked? Let me see: I can't tell—I didn't see her, for it was as if she had rushed straight into my arms at once and come so close to me that I couldn't make out her features at all. And she left her impression on the air behind her. I can still see her standing there. [He goes toward the door and makes a gesture as if putting his arm around somebody] Whew! [He makes a gesture as if he had pricked his finger] There are pins in her waist. She is of the kind that stings!

MME. CATHERINE. Oh, you are crazy, you with your ladies!

MAURICE. Yes, it's craziness, that's what it is. But do you know, Madame Catherine, I am going before she comes back, or else, or else—Oh, that woman is horrible!

MME. CATHERINE. Are you afraid?

MAURICE. Yes, I am afraid for myself, and also for some others.

MME. CATHERINE. Well, go then.

MAURICE. She seemed to suck herself out through the door, and in her wake rose a little whirlwind that dragged me along—Yes, you may laugh, but can't you see that the palm over there on the buffet is still shaking? She's the very devil of a woman!

MME. CATHERINE. Oh, get out of here, man, before you lose all your reason.

MAURICE. I want to go, but I cannot—Do you believe in fate, Madame Catherine?

MME. CATHERINE. No, I believe in a good God, who protects us against evil powers if we ask Him in the right way.

MAURICE. So there are evil powers after all! I think I can hear them in the hallway now.

MME. CATHERINE. Yes, her clothes rustle as when the clerk tears off a piece of linen for you. Get away now—through the kitchen.

(MAURICE rushes toward the kitchen door, where he bumps into EMILE.)

EMILE. I beg your pardon. [He retires the way he came.]

ADOLPHE. [Comes in first; after him HENRIETTE] Why, there's Maurice. How are you? Let me introduce this lady here to my oldest and best friend. Mademoiselle Henriette—Monsieur Maurice.

MAURICE. [Saluting stiffly] Pleased to meet you.

HENRIETTA. We have seen each other before.

ADOLPHE. Is that so? When, if I may ask?

MAURICE. A moment ago. Right here.

ADOLPHE. O-oh!—But now you must stay and have a chat with us.

MAURICE. [After a glance at MME. CATHERINE] If I only had time.

ADOLPHE. Take the time. And we won't be sitting here very long.

HENRIETTE. I won't interrupt, if you have to talk business.

MAURICE. The only business we have is so bad that we don't want to talk of it.

HENRIETTE. Then we'll talk of something else. [Takes the hat away from MAURICE and hangs it up] Now be nice, and let me become acquainted with the great author.

MME. CATHERINE signals to MAURICE, who doesn't notice her.

ADOLPHE. That's right, Henriette, you take charge of him. [They seat themselves at one of the tables.]

HENRIETTE. [To MAURICE] You certainly have a good friend in Adolphe, Monsieur Maurice. He never talks of anything but you, and in such a way that I feel myself rather thrown in the background.

ADOLPHE. You don't say so! Well, Henriette on her side never leaves me in peace about you, Maurice. She has read your works, and she is always wanting to know where you got this and where that. She has been questioning me about your looks, your age, your tastes. I have, in a word, had you for breakfast, dinner, and supper. It has almost seemed as if the three of us were living together.

MAURICE. [To HENRIETTE] Heavens, why didn't you come over here and have a look at this wonder of wonders? Then your curiosity could have been satisfied in a trice.

HENRIETTE. Adolphe didn't want it.

(ADOLPHE looks embarrassed.)

HENRIETTE. Not that he was jealous—

MAURICE. And why should he be, when he knows that my feelings are tied up elsewhere?

HENRIETTE. Perhaps he didn't trust the stability of your feelings.

MAURICE. I can't understand that, seeing that I am notorious for my constancy.

ADOLPHE. Well, it wasn't that—

HENRIETTE. [Interrupting him] Perhaps that is because you have not faced the fiery ordeal—

ADOLPHE. Oh, you don't know—

HENRIETTE. [Interrupting]—for the world has not yet beheld a faithful man.

MAURICE. Then it's going to behold one.

HENRIETTE. Where?

MAURICE. Here.

(HENRIETTE laughs.)

ADOLPHE. Well, that's going it—

HENRIETTE. [Interrupting him and directing herself continuously to MAURICE] Do you think I ever trust my dear Adolphe more than a month at a time?

MAURICE. I have no right to question your lack of confidence, but I can guarantee that Adolphe is faithful.

HENRIETTE. You don't need to do so—my tongue is just running away with me, and I have to take back a lot—not only for fear of feeling less generous than you, but because it is the truth. It is a bad habit I have of only seeing the ugly side of things, and I keep it up although I know better. But if I had a chance to be with you two for some time, then your company would make me good once more. Pardon me, Adolphe! [She puts her hand against his cheek.]

ADOLPHE. You are always wrong in your talk and right in your actions. What you really think—that I don't know.

HENRIETTE. Who does know that kind of thing?

MAURICE. Well, if we had to answer for our thoughts, who could then clear himself?

HENRIETTE. Do you also have evil thoughts?

MAURICE. Certainly; just as I commit the worst kind of cruelties in my dreams.

HENRIETTE. Oh, when you are dreaming, of course—Just think of it—

No, I am ashamed of telling—

MAURICE. Go on, go on!

HENRIETTE. Last night I dreamt that I was coolly dissecting the muscles on Adolphe's breast—you see, I am a sculptor—and he, with his usual kindness, made no resistance, but helped me instead with the worst places, as he knows more anatomy than I.

MAURICE. Was he dead?

HENRIETTE. No, he was living.

MAURICE. But that's horrible! And didn't it make YOU suffer?

HENRIETTE. Not at all, and that astonished me most, for I am rather sensitive to other people's sufferings. Isn't that so, Adolphe?

ADOLPHE. That's right. Rather abnormally so, in fact, and not the least when animals are concerned.

MAURICE. And I, on the other hand, am rather callous toward the sufferings both of myself and others.

ADOLPHE. Now he is not telling the truth about himself. Or what do you say, Madame Catherine?

MME. CATHERINE. I don't know of anybody with a softer heart than Monsieur Maurice. He came near calling in the police because I didn't give the goldfish fresh water—those over there on the buffet. Just look at them: it is as if they could hear what I am saying.

MAURICE. Yes, here we are making ourselves out as white as angels, and yet we are, taking it all in all, capable of any kind of polite atrocity the moment glory, gold, or women are concerned—So you are a sculptor, Mademoiselle Henriette?

HENRIETTE. A bit of one. Enough to do a bust. And to do one of you— which has long been my cherished dream—I hold myself quite capable.

MAURICE. Go ahead! That dream at least need not be long in coming true.

HENRIETTE. But I don't want to fix your features in my mind until this evening's success is over. Not until then will you have become what you should be.

MAURICE. How sure you are of victory!

HENRIETTE. Yes, it is written on your face that you are going to win this battle, and I think you must feel that yourself.

MAURICE. Why do you think so?

HENRIETTE. Because I can feel it. This morning I was ill, you know, and now I am well.

(ADOLPHE begins to look depressed.)

MAURICE. [Embarrassed] Listen, I have a single ticket left—only one. I place it at your disposal, Adolphe.

ADOLPHE. Thank you, but I surrender it to Henriette.

HENRIETTE. But that wouldn't do?

ADOLPHE. Why not? And I never go to the theatre anyhow, as I cannot stand the heat.

HENRIETTE. But you will come and take us home at least after the show is over.

ADOLPHE. If you insist on it. Otherwise Maurice has to come back here, where we shall all be waiting for him.

MAURICE. You can just as well take the trouble of meeting us. In fact, I ask, I beg you to do so—And if you don't want to wait outside the theatre, you can meet us at the Auberge des Adrets— That's settled then, isn't it?

ADOLPHE. Wait a little. You have a way of settling things to suit yourself, before other people have a chance to consider them.

MAURICE. What is there to consider—whether you are to see your lady home or not?

ADOLPHE. You never know what may be involved in a simple act like that, but I have a sort of premonition.

HENRIETTE. Hush, hush, hush! Don't talk of spooks while the sun is shining. Let him come or not, as it pleases him. We can always find our way back here.

ADOLPHE. [Rising] Well, now I have to leave you—model, you know. Good-bye, both of you. And good luck to you, Maurice. To-morrow you will be out on the right side. Good-bye, Henriette.

HENRIETTE. Do you really have to go?

ADOLPHE. I must.

MAURICE. Good-bye then. We'll meet later.

(ADOLPHE goes out, saluting MME. CATHERINE in passing.)

HENRIETTE. Think of it, that we should meet at last!

MAURICE. Do you find anything remarkable in that?

HENRIETTE. It looks as if it had to happen, for Adolphe has done his best to prevent it.

MAURICE. Has he?

HENRIETTE. Oh, you must have noticed it.

MAURICE. I have noticed it, but why should you mention it?

HENRIETTE. I had to.

MAURICE. No, and I don't have to tell you that I wanted to run away through the kitchen in order to avoid meeting you and was stopped by a guest who closed the door in front of me.

HENRIETTE. Why do you tell me about it now?

MAURICE. I don't know.

(MME. CATHERINE upsets a number of glasses and bottles.)

MAURICE. That's all right, Madame Catherine. There's nothing to be afraid of.

HENRIETTE. Was that meant as a signal or a warning?

MAURICE. Probably both.

HENRIETTE. Do they take me for a locomotive that has to have flagmen ahead of it?

MAURICE. And switchmen! The danger is always greatest at the switches.

HENRIETTE. How nasty you can be!

MME. CATHERINE. Monsieur Maurice isn't nasty at all. So far nobody has been kinder than he to those that love him and trust in him.

MAURICE. Sh, sh, sh!

HENRIETTE. [To MAURICE] The old lady is rather impertinent.

MAURICE. We can walk over to the boulevard, if you care to do so.

HENRIETTE. With pleasure. This is not the place for me. I can just feel their hatred clawing at me. [Goes out.]

MAURICE. [Starts after her] Good-bye, Madame Catherine.

MME. CATHERINE. A moment! May I speak a word to you, Monsieur Maurice?

MAURICE. [Stops unwillingly] What is it?

MME. CATHERINE. Don't do it! Don't do it!

MAURICE. What?

MME. CATHERINE. Don't do it!

MAURICE. Don't be scared. This lady is not my kind, but she interests me. Or hardly that even.

MME. CATHERINE, Don't trust yourself!

MAURICE. Yes, I do trust myself. Good-bye. [Goes out.]

(Curtain.)

ACT II

FIRST SCENE

(THE Auberge des Adrets: a café in sixteenth century style, with a suggestion of stage effect. Tables and easy-chairs are scattered in corners and nooks. The walls are decorated with armour and weapons. Along the ledge of the wainscoting stand glasses and jugs.)

(MAURICE and HENRIETTE are in evening dress and sit facing each other at a table on which stands a bottle of champagne and three filled glasses. The third glass is placed at that side of the table which is nearest the background, and there an easy-chair is kept ready for the still missing "third man.")

MAURICE. [Puts his watch in front of himself on the table] If he doesn't get here within the next five minutes, he isn't coming at all. And suppose in the meantime we drink with his ghost. [Touches the third glass with the rim of his own.]

HENRIETTE. [Doing the same] Here's to you, Adolphe!

MAURICE. He won't come.

HENRIETTE. He will come.

MAURICE. He won't.

HENRIETTE. He will.

MAURICE. What an evening! What a wonderful day! I can hardly grasp that a new life has begun. Think only: the manager believes that I may count on no less than one hundred thousand francs. I'll spend twenty thousand on a villa outside the city. That leaves me eighty thousand. I won't be able to take it all in until to-morrow, for I am tired, tired, tired. [Sinks back into the chair] Have you ever felt really happy?

HENRIETTE. Never. How does it feel?

MAURICE. I don't quite know how to put it. I cannot express it, but I seem chiefly to be thinking of the chagrin of my enemies. It isn't nice, but that's the way it is.

HENRIETTE. Is it happiness to be thinking of one's enemies?

MAURICE. Why, the victor has to count his killed and wounded enemies in order to gauge the extent of his victory.

HENRIETTE. Are you as bloodthirsty as all that?

MAURICE. Perhaps not. But when you have felt the pressure of other people's heels on your chest for years, it must be pleasant to shake off the enemy and draw a full breath at last.

HENRIETTE. Don't you find it strange that yon are sitting here, alone with me, an insignificant girl practically unknown to you— and on an evening like this, when you ought to have a craving to show yourself like a triumphant hero to all the people, on the boulevards, in the big restaurants?

MAURICE. Of course, it's rather funny, but it feels good to be here, and your company is all I care for.

HENRIETTE. You don't look very hilarious.

MAURICE. No, I feel rather sad, and I should like to weep a little.

HENRIETTE. What is the meaning of that?

MAURICE. It is fortune conscious of its own nothingness and waiting for misfortune to appear.

HENRIETTE. Oh my, how sad! What is it you are missing anyhow?

MAURICE. I miss the only thing that gives value to life.

HENRIETTE. So you love her no longer then?

MAURICE. Not in the way I understand love. Do you think she has read my play, or that she wants to see it? Oh, she is so good, so self-sacrificing and considerate, but to go out with me for a night's fun she would regard as sinful. Once I treated her to champagne, you know, and instead of feeling happy over it, she picked up the wine list to see what it cost. And when she read the price, she wept—wept because Marion was in need of new stockings. It is beautiful, of course: it is touching, if you please. But I can get no pleasure out of it. And I do want a little pleasure before life runs out. So far I have had nothing but privation, but now, now—life is beginning for me. [The clock strikes twelve] Now begins a new day, a new era!

HENRIETTE. Adolphe is not coming.

MAURICE. No, now he won't, come. And now it is too late to go back to the Crêmerie.

HENRIETTE. But they are waiting for you.

MAURICE. Let them wait. They have made me promise to come, and I take back my promise. Are you longing to go there?

HENRIETTE. On the contrary!

MAURICE. Will you keep me company then?

HENRIETTE. With pleasure, if you care to have me.

MAURICE. Otherwise I shouldn't be asking you. It is strange, you know, that the victor's wreath seems worthless if you can't place it at the feet of some woman—that everything seems worthless when you have not a woman.

HENRIETTE. You don't need to be without a woman—you?

MAURICE. Well, that's the question.

HENRIETTE. Don't you know that a man is irresistible in his hour of success and fame?

MAURICE. No, I don't know, for I have had no experience of it.

HENRIETTE. You are a queer sort! At this moment, when you are the most envied man in Paris, you sit here and brood. Perhaps your conscience is troubling you because you have neglected that invitation to drink chicory coffee with the old lady over at the milk shop?

MAURICE. Yes, my conscience is troubling me on that score, and even here I am aware of their resentment, their hurt feelings, their well-grounded anger. My comrades in distress had the right to demand my presence this evening. The good Madame Catherine had a privileged claim on my success, from which a glimmer of hope was to spread over the poor fellows who have not yet succeeded. And I have robbed them of their faith in me. I can hear the vows they have been making: "Maurice will come, for he is a good fellow; he doesn't despise us, and he never fails to keep his word." Now I have made them forswear themselves.

(While he is still speaking, somebody in the next room has begun to play the finale of Beethoven's Sonata in D-minor (Op. 31, No. 3). The allegretto is first played piano, then more forte, and at last passionately, violently, with complete abandon.)

MAURICE. Who can be playing at this time of the night?

HENRIETTE. Probably some nightbirds of the same kind as we. But listen! Your presentation of the case is not correct. Remember that Adolphe promised to meet us here. We waited for him, and he failed to keep his promise. So that you are not to blame—

MAURICE. You think so? While you are speaking, I believe you, but when you stop, my conscience begins again. What have you in that package?

HENRIETTE. Oh, it is only a laurel wreath that I meant to send up to the stage, but I had no chance to do so. Let me give it to you now—it is said to have a cooling effect on burning foreheads. [She rises and crowns him with the wreath; then she kisses him on the forehead] Hail to the victor!

MAURICE. Don't!

HENRIETTE. [Kneeling] Hail to the King!

MAURICE. [Rising] No, now you scare me.

HENRIETTE. You timid man! You of little faith who are afraid of fortune even! Who robbed you of your self-assurance and turned you into a dwarf?

MAURICE. A dwarf? Yes, you are right. I am not working up in the clouds, like a giant, with crashing and roaring, but I forge my weapons deep down in the silent heart of the mountain. You think that my modesty shrinks before the victor's wreath. On the contrary, I despise it: it is not enough for me. You think I am afraid of that ghost with its jealous green eyes which sits over there and keeps watch on my feelings—the strength of which you don't suspect. Away, ghost! [He brushes the third, untouched glass off the table] Away with you, you superfluous third person—you absent one who has lost your rights, if you ever had any. You stayed away from the field of battle because you knew yourself already beaten. As I crush this glass under my foot, so I will crush the image of yourself which you have reared in a temple no longer yours.

HENRIETTE. Good! That's the way! Well spoken, my hero!

MAURICE. Now I have sacrificed my best friend, my most faithful helper, on your altar, Astarte! Are you satisfied?

HENRIETTE. Astarte is a pretty name, and I'll keep it—I think you love me, Maurice.

MAURICE. Of course I do—Woman of evil omen, you who stir up man's courage with your scent of blood, whence do you come and where do you lead me? I loved you before I saw you, for I trembled when I heard them speak of you. And when I saw you in the doorway, your soul poured itself into mine. And when you left, I could still feel your presence in my arms. I wanted to flee from you, but something held me back, and this evening we have been driven together as the prey is driven into the hunter's net. Whose is the fault? Your friend's, who pandered for us!

HENRIETTE. Fault or no fault: what does it matter, and what does it mean?—Adolphe has been at fault in not bringing us together before. He is guilty of having stolen from us two weeks of bliss, to which he had no right himself. I am jealous of him on your behalf. I hate him because he has cheated you out of your mistress. I should like to blot him from the host of the living, and his memory with him—wipe him out of the past even, make him unmade, unborn!

MAURICE. Well, we'll bury him beneath our own memories. We'll cover him with leaves and branches far out in the wild woods, and then we'll pile stone on top of the mound so that he will never look up again. [Raising his glass] Our fate is sealed. Woe unto us! What will come next?

HENRIETTE. Next comes the new era—What have you in that package?

MAURICE. I cannot remember.

HENRIETTE. [Opens the package and takes out a tie and a pair of gloves] That tie is a fright! It must have cost at least fifty centimes.

MAURICE. [Snatching the things away from her] Don't you touch them!

HENRIETTE. They are from her?

MAURICE. Yes, they are.

HENRIETTE. Give them to me.

MAURICE. No, she's better than we, better than everybody else.

HENRIETTE. I don't believe it. She is simply stupider and stingier. One who weeps because you order champagne—

MAURICE. When the child was without stockings. Yes, she is a good woman.

HENRIETTE. Philistine! You'll never be an artist. But I am an artist, and I'll make a bust of you with a shopkeeper's cap instead of the laurel wreath— Her name is Jeanne?

MAURICE. How do you know?

HENRIETTE. Why, that's the name of all housekeepers.

MAURICE. Henriette!

(HENRIETTE takes the tie and the gloves and throws them into the fireplace.)

MAURICE. [Weakly] Astarte, now you demand the sacrifice of women. You shall have them, but if you ask for innocent children, too, then I'll send you packing.

HENRIETTE. Can you tell me what it is that binds you to me?

MAURICE. If I only knew, I should be able to tear myself away. But I believe it must be those qualities which you have and I lack. I believe that the evil within you draws me with the irresistible lure of novelty.

HENRIETTE. Have you ever committed a crime?

MAURICE. No real one. Have you?

HENRIETTE. Yes.

MAURICE. Well, how did you find it?

HENRIETTE. It was greater than to perform a good deed, for by that we are placed on equality with others; it was greater than to perform some act of heroism, for by that we are raised above others and rewarded. That crime placed me outside and beyond life, society, and my fellow-beings. Since then I am living only a partial life, a sort of dream life, and that's why reality never gets a hold on me.

MAURICE. What was it you did?

HENRIETTE. I won't tell, for then you would get scared again.

MAURICE. Can you never be found out?

HENRIETTE. Never. But that does not prevent me from seeing, frequently, the five stones at the Place de Roquette, where the scaffold used to stand; and for this reason I never dare to open a pack of cards, as I always turn up the five-spot of diamonds.

MAURICE. Was it that kind of a crime?

HENRIETTE. Yes, it was that kind.

MAURICE. Of course, it's horrible, but it is interesting. Have you no conscience?

HENRIETTE. None, but I should be grateful if you would talk of something else.

MAURICE. Suppose we talk of—love?

HENRIETTE. Of that you don't talk until it is over.

MAURICE. Have you been in love with Adolphe?

HENRIETTE. I don't know. The goodness of his nature drew me like some beautiful, all but vanished memory of childhood. Yet there was much about his person that offended my eye, so that I had to spend a long time retouching, altering, adding, subtracting, before I could make a presentable figure of him. When he talked, I could notice that he had learned from you, and the lesson was often badly digested and awkwardly applied. You can imagine then how miserable the copy must appear now, when I am permitted to study the original. That's why he was afraid of having us two meet; and when it did happen, he understood at once that his time was up.

MAURICE. Poor Adolphe!

HENRIETTE. I feel sorry for him, too, as I know he must be suffering beyond all bounds—

MAURICE. Sh! Somebody is coming.

HENRIETTE. I wonder if it could be he?

MAURICE. That would be unbearable.

HENRIETTE. No, it isn't he, but if it had been, how do you think the situation would have shaped itself?

MAURICE. At first he would have been a little sore at you because he had made a mistake in regard to the meeting-place—and tried to find us in several other cafes—but his soreness would have changed into pleasure at finding us—and seeing that we had not deceived him. And in the joy at having wronged us by his suspicions, he would love both of us. And so it would make him happy to notice that we had become such good friends. It had always been his dream—hm! he is making the speech now—his dream that the three of us should form a triumvirate that could set the world a great example of friendship asking for nothing—"Yes, I trust you, Maurice, partly because you are my friend, and partly because your feelings are tied up elsewhere."

HENRIETTE. Bravo! You must have been in a similar situation before, or you couldn't give such a lifelike picture of it. Do you know that Adolphe is just that kind of a third person who cannot enjoy his mistress without having his friend along?

MAURICE. That's why I had to be called in to entertain you—Hush! There is somebody outside—It must be he.

HENRIETTE. No, don't you know these are the hours when ghosts walk, and then you can see so many things, and hear them also. To keep awake at night, when you ought to be sleeping, has for me the same charm as a crime: it is to place oneself above and beyond the laws of nature.

MAURICE. But the punishment is fearful—I am shivering or quivering, with cold or with fear.

HENRIETTE. [Wraps her opera cloak about him] Put this on. It will make you warm.

MAURICE. That's nice. It is as if I were inside of your skin, as if my body had been melted up by lack of sleep and were being remoulded in your shape. I can feel the moulding process going on. But I am also growing a new soul, new thoughts, and here, where your bosom has left an impression, I can feel my own beginning to bulge.

(During this entire scene, the pianist in the next room has been practicing the Sonata in D-minor, sometimes pianissimo, sometimes wildly fortissimo; now and then he has kept silent for a little while, and at other times nothing has been heard but a part of the finale: bars 96 to 107.)

MAURICE. What a monster, to sit there all night practicing on the piano. It gives me a sick feeling. Do you know what I propose? Let us drive out to the Bois de Boulogne and take breakfast in the Pavilion, and see the sun rise over the lakes.

HENRIETTE. Bully!

MAURICE. But first of all I must arrange to have my mail and the morning papers sent out by messenger to the Pavilion. Tell me, Henriette: shall we invite Adolphe?

HENRIETTE. Oh, that's going too far! But why not? The ass can also be harnessed to the triumphal chariot. Let him come. [They get up.]

MAURICE. [Taking off the cloak] Then I'll ring.

HENRIETTE. Wait a moment! [Throws herself into his arms.]

(Curtain.)

SECOND SCENE

(A large, splendidly furnished restaurant room in the Bois de Boulogne. It is richly carpeted and full of mirrors, easy-chairs, and divans. There are glass doors in the background, and beside them windows overlooking the lakes. In the foreground a table is spread, with flowers in the centre, bowls full of fruit, wine in decanters, oysters on platters, many different kinds of wine glasses, and two lighted candelabra. On the right there is a round table full of newspapers and telegrams.)

(MAURICE and HENRIETTE are sitting opposite each other at this small table.)

(The sun is just rising outside.)

MAURICE. There is no longer any doubt about it. The newspapers tell me it is so, and these telegrams congratulate me on my success. This is the beginning of a new life, and my fate is wedded to yours by this night, when you were the only one to share my hopes and my triumph. From your hand I received the laurel, and it seems to me as if everything had come from you.

HENRIETTE. What a wonderful night! Have we been dreaming, or is this something we have really lived through?

MAURICE. [Rising] And what a morning after such a night! I feel as if it were the world's first day that is now being illumined by the rising sun. Only this minute was the earth created and stripped of those white films that are now floating off into space. There lies the Garden of Eden in the rosy light of dawn, and here is the first human couple—Do you know, I am so happy I could cry at the thought that all mankind is not equally happy—Do you hear that distant murmur as of ocean waves beating against a rocky shore, as of winds sweeping through a forest? Do you know what it is? It is Paris whispering my name. Do you see the columns of smoke that rise skyward in thousands and tens of thousands? They are the fires burning on my altars, and if that be not so, then it must become so, for I will it. At this moment all the telegraph instruments of Europe are clicking out my name. The Oriental Express is carrying the newspapers to the Far East, toward the rising sun; and the ocean steamers are carrying them to the utmost West. The earth is mine, and for that reason it is beautiful. Now I should like to have wings for us two, so that we might rise from here and fly far, far away, before anybody can soil my happiness, before envy has a chance to wake me out of my dream—for it is probably a dream!

HENRIETTE. [Holding out her hand to him] Here you can feel that you are not dreaming.

MAURICE. It is not a dream, but it has been one. As a poor young man, you know, when I was walking in the woods down there, and looked up to this Pavilion, it looked to me like a fairy castle, and always my thoughts carried me up to this room, with the balcony outside and the heavy curtains, as to a place of supreme bliss. To be sitting here in company with a beloved woman and see the sun rise while the candles were still burning in the candelabra: that was the most audacious dream of my youth. Now it has come true, and now I have no more to ask of life—Do you want to die now, together with me?

HENRIETTE. No, you fool! Now I want to begin living.

MAURICE. [Rising] To live: that is to suffer! Now comes reality. I can hear his steps on the stairs. He is panting with alarm, and his heart is beating with dread of having lost what it holds most precious. Can you believe me if I tell you that Adolphe is under this roof? Within a minute he will be standing in the middle of this floor.

HENRIETTE. [Alarmed] It was a stupid trick to ask him to come here, and I am already regretting it—Well, we shall see anyhow if your forecast of the situation proves correct.

MAURICE. Oh, it is easy to be mistaken about a person's feelings.

(The HEAD WAITER enters with a card.)

MAURICE. Ask the gentleman to step in. [To HENRIETTE] I am afraid we'll regret this.

HENRIETTE. Too late to think of that now—Hush!

(ADOLPHE enters, pale and hollow-eyed.)

MAURICE. [Trying to speak unconcernedly] There you are! What became of you last night?

ADOLPHE. I looked for you at the Hotel des Arrets and waited a whole hour.

MAURICE. So you went to the wrong place. We were waiting several hours for you at the Auberge des Adrets, and we are still waiting for you, as you see.

ADOLPHE. [Relieved] Thank heaven!

HENRIETTE. Good morning, Adolphe. You are always expecting the worst and worrying yourself needlessly. I suppose you imagined that we wanted to avoid your company. And though you see that we sent for you, you are still thinking yourself superfluous.

ADOLPHE. Pardon me: I was wrong, but the night was dreadful.

(They sit down. Embarrassed silence follows.)

HENRIETTE. [To ADOLPHE] Well, are you not going to congratulate Maurice on his great success?

ADOLPHE. Oh, yes! Your success is the real thing, and envy itself cannot deny it. Everything is giving way before you, and even I have a sense of my own smallness in your presence.

MAURICE. Nonsense!—Henriette, are you not going to offer Adolphe a glass of wine?

ADOLPHE. Thank you, not for me—nothing at all!

HENRIETTE. [To ADOLPHE] What's the matter with you? Are you ill?

ADOLPHE. Not yet, but—

HENRIETTE. Your eyes—

ADOLPHE. What of them?

MAURICE. What happened at the Crêmerie last night? I suppose they are angry with me?

ADOLPHE. Nobody is angry with you, but your absence caused a depression which it hurt me to watch. But nobody was angry with you, believe me. Your friends understood, and they regarded your failure to come with sympathetic forbearance. Madame Catherine herself defended you and proposed your health. We all rejoiced in your success as if it had been our own.

HENRIETTE. Well, those are nice people! What good friends you have, Maurice.

MAURICE. Yes, better than I deserve.

ADOLPHE. Nobody has better friends than he deserves, and you are a man greatly blessed in his friends—Can't you feel how the air is softened to-day by all the kind thoughts and wishes that stream toward you from a thousand breasts?

(MAURICE rises in order to hide his emotion.)

ADOLPHE. From a thousand breasts that you have rid of the nightmare that had been crushing them during a lifetime. Humanity had been slandered— and you have exonerated it: that's why men feel grateful toward you. To-day they are once more holding their heads high and saying: You see, we are a little better than our reputation after all. And that thought makes them better.

(HENRIETTE tries to hide her emotion.)

ADOLPHE. Am I in the way? Just let me warm myself a little in your sunshine, Maurice, and then I'll go.

MAURICE. Why should you go when you have only just arrived?

ADOLPHE. Why? Because I have seen what I need not have seen; because I know now that my hour is past. [Pause] That you sent for me, I take as an expression of thoughtfulness, a notice of what has happened, a frankness that hurts less than deceit. You hear that I think well of my fellow-beings, and this I have learned from you, Maurice. [Pause] But, my friend, a few moments ago I passed through the Church of St. Germain, and there I saw a woman and a child. I am not wishing that you had seen them, for what has happened cannot be altered, but if you gave a thought or a word to them before you set them adrift on the waters of the great city, then you could enjoy your happiness undisturbed. And now I bid you good-by.

HENRIETTE. Why must you go?

ADOLPHE. And you ask that? Do you want me to tell you?

HENRIETTE. No, I don't.

ADOLPHE. Good-by then! [Goes out.]

MAURICE. The Fall: and lo! "they knew that they were naked."

HENRIETTE. What a difference between this scene and the one we imagined! He is better than we.

MAURICE. It seems to me now as if all the rest were better than we.

HENRIETTE. Do you see that the sun has vanished behind clouds, and that the woods have lost their rose colour?

MAURICE. Yes, I see, and the blue lake has turned black. Let us flee to some place where the sky is always blue and the trees are always green.

HENRIETTE. Yes, let us—but without any farewells.

MAURICE. No, with farewells.

HENRIETTE. We were to fly. You spoke of wings—and your feet are of lead. I am not jealous, but if you go to say farewell and get two pairs of arms around your neck—then you can't tear yourself away.

MAURICE. Perhaps you are right, but only one pair of little arms is needed to hold me fast.

HENRIETTE. It is the child that holds you then, and not the woman?

MAURICE. It is the child.

HENRIETTE. The child! Another woman's child! And for the sake of it I am to suffer. Why must that child block the way where I want to pass, and must pass?

MAURICE. Yes, why? It would be better if it had never existed.

HENRIETTE. [Walks excitedly back and forth] Indeed! But now it does exist. Like a rock on the road, a rock set firmly in the ground, immovable, so that it upsets the carriage.

MAURICE. The triumphal chariot!—The ass is driven to death, but the rock remains. Curse it! [Pause.]

HENRIETTE. There is nothing to do.

MAURICE. Yes, we must get married, and then our child will make us forget the other one.

HENRIETTE. This will kill this!

MAURICE. Kill! What kind of word is that?

HENRIETTE. [Changing tone] Your child will kill our love.

MAURICE. No, girl, our love will kill whatever stands in its way, but it will not be killed.

HENRIETTE. [Opens a deck of cards lying on the mantlepiece] Look at it! Five-spot of diamonds—the scaffold! Can it be possible that our fates are determined in advance? That our thoughts are guided as if through pipes to the spot for which they are bound, without chance for us to stop them? But I don't want it, I don't want it!—Do you realise that I must go to the scaffold if my crime should be discovered?

MAURICE. Tell me about your crime. Now is the time for it.

HENRIETTE. No, I should regret it afterward, and you would despise me—no, no, no!—Have you ever heard that a person could be hated to death? Well, my father incurred the hatred of my mother and my sisters, and he melted away like wax before a fire. Ugh! Let us talk of something else. And, above all, let us get away. The air is poisoned here. To-morrow your laurels will be withered, the triumph will be forgotten, and in a week another triumphant hero will hold the public attention. Away from here, to work for new victories! But first of all, Maurice, you must embrace your child and provide for its immediate future. You don't have to see the mother at all.

MAURICE. Thank you! Your good heart does you honour, and I love you doubly when you show the kindness you generally hide.

HENRIETTE. And then you go to the Crêmerie and say good-by to the old lady and your friends. Leave no unsettled business behind to make your mind heavy on our trip.

MAURICE. I'll clear up everything, and to-night we meet at the railroad station.

HENRIETTE. Agreed! And then: away from here—away toward the sea and the sun!

(Curtain.)

ACT III

FIRST SCENE

(IN the Crêmerie. The gas is lit. MME. CATHERINE is seated at the counter, ADOLPHE at a table.)

MME. CATHERINE. Such is life, Monseiur Adolphe. But you young ones are always demanding too much, and then you come here and blubber over it afterward.

ADOLPHE. No, it isn't that. I reproach nobody, and I am as fond as ever of both of them. But there is one thing that makes me sick at heart. You see, I thought more of Maurice than of anybody else; so much that I wouldn't have grudged him anything that could give him pleasure—but now I have lost him, and it hurts me worse than the loss of her. I have lost both of them, and so my loneliness is made doubly painful. And then there is still something else which I have not yet been able to clear up.

MME. CATHERINE. Don't brood so much. Work and divert yourself. Now, for instance, do you ever go to church?

ADOLPHE. What should I do there?

MME. CATHERINE. Oh, there's so much to look at, and then there is the music. There is nothing commonplace about it, at least.

ADOLPHE. Perhaps not. But I don't belong to that fold, I guess, for it never stirs me to any devotion. And then, Madame Catherine, faith is a gift, they tell me, and I haven't got it yet.

MME. CATHERINE. Well, wait till you get it—But what is this I heard a while ago? Is it true that you have sold a picture in London for a high price, and that you have got a medal?

ADOLPHE. Yes, it's true.

MME. CATHERINE. Merciful heavens!—and not a word do you say about it?

ADOLPHE. I am afraid of fortune, and besides it seems almost worthless to me at this moment. I am afraid of it as of a spectre: it brings disaster to speak of having seen it.

MME. CATHERINE. You're a queer fellow, and that's what you have always been.

ADOLPHE. Not queer at all, but I have seen so much misfortune come in the wake of fortune, and I have seen how adversity brings out true friends, while none but false ones appear in the hour of success—You asked me if I ever went to church, and I answered evasively. This morning I stepped into the Church of St. Germain without really knowing why I did so. It seemed as if I were looking for somebody in there—somebody to whom I could silently offer my gratitude. But I found nobody. Then I dropped a gold coin in the poor-box. It was all I could get out of my church-going, and that was rather commonplace, I should say.

MME. CATHERINE. It was always something; and then it was fine to think of the poor after having heard good news.

ADOLPHE. It was neither fine nor anything else: it was something I did because I couldn't help myself. But something more occurred while I was in the church. I saw Maurice's girl friend, Jeanne, and her child. Struck down, crushed by his triumphal chariot, they seemed aware of the full extent of their misfortune.

MME. CATHERINE. Well, children, I don't know in what kind of shape you keep your consciences. But how a decent fellow, a careful and considerate man like Monsieur Maurice, can all of a sudden desert a woman and her child, that is something I cannot explain.

ADOLPHE. Nor can I explain it, and he doesn't seem to understand it himself. I met them this morning, and everything appeared quite natural to them, quite proper, as if they couldn't imagine anything else. It was as if they had been enjoying the satisfaction of a good deed or the fulfilment of a sacred duty. There are things, Madame Catherine, that we cannot explain, and for this reason it is not for us to judge. And besides, you saw how it happened. Maurice felt the danger in the air. I foresaw it and tried to prevent their meeting. Maurice wanted to run away from it, but nothing helped. Why, it was as if a plot had been laid by some invisible power, and as if they had been driven by guile into each other's arms. Of course, I am disqualified in this case, but I wouldn't hesitate to pronounce a verdict of "not guilty."

MME. CATHERINE. Well, now, to be able to forgive as you do, that's what I call religion.

ADOLPHE. Heavens, could it be that I am religious without knowing it.

MME. CATHERINE. But then, to *let* oneself be driven or tempted into evil, as Monsieur Maurice has done, means weakness or bad character. And if you feel your strength failing you, then you ask for help, and then you get it. But he was too conceited to do that—Who is this coming? The Abbé, I think.

ADOLPHE. What does he want here?

ABBÉ. [Enters] Good evening, madame. Good evening, Monsieur.

MME. CATHERINE. Can I be of any service?

ABBÉ. Has Monsieur Maurice, the author, been here to-day?

MME. CATHERINE. Not to-day. His play has just been put on, and that is probably keeping him busy.

ABBÉ. I have—sad news to bring him. Sad in several respects.

MME. CATHERINE. May I ask of what kind?

ABBÉ. Yes, it's no secret. The daughter he had with that girl, Jeanne, is dead.

MME. CATHERINE. Dead!

ADOLPHE. Marion dead!

ABBÉ. Yes, she died suddenly this morning without any previous illness.

MME. CATHERINE. O Lord, who can tell Thy ways!

ABBÉ. The mother's grief makes it necessary that Monsieur Maurice look after her, so we must try to find him. But first a question in confidence: do you know whether Monsieur Maurice was fond of the child, or was indifferent to it?

MME. CATHERINE. If he was fond of Marion? Why, all of us know how he loved her.

ADOLPHE. There's no doubt about that.

ABBÉ. I am glad to hear it, and it settles the matter so far as I am concerned.

MME. CATHERINE. Has there been any doubt about it?

ABBÉ. Yes, unfortunately. It has even been rumoured in the neighbourhood that he had abandoned the child and its mother in order to go away with a strange woman. In a few hours this rumour has grown into definite accusations, and at the same time the feeling against him has risen to such a point that his life is threatened and he is being called a murderer.

MME. CATHERINE. Good God, what is *this*? What does it mean?

ABBÉ. Now I'll tell you my opinion—I am convinced that the man is innocent on this score, and the mother feels as certain about it as I do. But appearances are against Monsieur Maurice, and I think he will find it rather hard to clear himself when the police come to question him.

ADOLPHE. Have the police got hold of the matter?

ABBÉ. Yea, the police have had to step in to protect him against all those ugly rumours and the rage of the people. Probably the Commissaire will be here soon.

MME. CATHERINE. [To ADOLPHE] There you see what happens when a man cannot tell the difference between good and evil, and when he trifles with vice. God will punish!

ADOLPHE. Then he is more merciless than man.

ABBÉ. What do you know about that?

ADOLPHE. Not very much, but I keep an eye on what happens—

ABBÉ. And you understand it also?

ADOLPHE. Not yet perhaps.

ABBÉ. Let us look more closely at the matter—Oh, here comes the Commissaire.

COMMISSAIRE. [Enters] Gentlemen—Madame Catherine—I have to trouble you for a moment with a few questions concerning Monsieur Maurice. As you have probably heard, he has become the object of a hideous rumour, which, by the by, I don't believe in.

MME. CATHERINE. None of us believes in it either.

COMMISSAIRE. That strengthens my own opinion, but for his own sake I must give him a chance to defend himself.

ABBÉ. That's right, and I guess he will find justice, although it may come hard.

COMMISSAIRE. Appearances are very much against him, but I have seen guiltless people reach the scaffold before their innocence was discovered. Let me tell you what there is against him. The little girl, Marion, being left alone by her mother, was secretly visited by the father, who seems to have made sure of the time when the child was to be found alone. Fifteen minutes after his visit the mother returned home and found the child dead. All this makes the position of the accused man very unpleasant—The post- mortem examination brought out no signs of violence or of poison, but the physicians admit the existence of new poisons that leave no traces behind them. To me all this is mere coincidence of the kind I frequently come across. But here's something that looks worse. Last night Monsieur Maurice was seen at the Auberge des Adrets in company with a strange lady. According to the waiter, they were talking about crimes. The Place de Roquette and the scaffold were both mentioned. A queer topic of conversation for a pair of lovers of good breeding and good social position! But even this may be passed over, as we know by experience that people who have been drinking and losing a lot of sleep seem inclined to dig up all the worst that lies at the bottom of their souls. Far more serious is the evidence given by the head waiter as to their champagne breakfast in the Bois de Boulogne this morning. He says that he heard them wish the life out of a child. The man is said to have remarked that, "It would be better if it had never existed." To which the woman replied: "Indeed! But now it does exist." And as they went on talking, these words occurred: "This will kill this!" And the answer was: "Kill! What kind of word is that?" And also: "The five-spot of diamonds, the scaffold, the Place de Roquette." All this, you see, will be hard to get out of, and so will the foreign journey planned for this evening. These are serious matters.

ADOLPHE. He is lost!

MME. CATHERINE. That's a dreadful story. One doesn't know what to believe.

ABBÉ. This is not the work of man. God have mercy on him!

ADOLPHE. He is in the net, and he will never get out of it.

MME. CATHERINE. He had no business to get in.

ADOLPHE. Do you begin to suspect him also, Madame Catherine?

MME. CATHERINE. Yes and no. I have got beyond having an opinion in this matter. Have you not seen angels turn into devils just as you turn your hand, and then become angels again?

COMMISSAIRE. It certainly does look queer. However, we'll have to wait and hear what explanations he can give. No one will be judged unheard. Good evening, gentlemen. Good evening, Madame Catherine. [Goes out.]

ABBÉ. This is not the work of man.

ADOLPHE. No, it looks as if demons had been at work for the undoing of man.

ABBÉ. It is either a punishment for secret misdeeds, or it is a terrible test.

JEANNE. [Enters, dressed in mourning] Good evening. Pardon me for asking, but have you seen Monsieur Maurice?

MME. CATHERINE. No, madame, but I think he may be here any minute. You haven't met him then since—

JEANNE. Not since this morning.

MME. CATHERINE. Let me tell you that I share in your great sorrow.

JEANNE. Thank you, madame. [To the ABBÉ] So you are here, Father.

ABBÉ. Yes, my child. I thought I might be of some use to you. And it was fortunate, as it gave me a chance to speak to the Commissaire.

JEANNE. The Commissaire! He doesn't suspect Maurice also, does he?

ABBÉ. No, he doesn't, and none of us here do. But appearances are against him in a most appalling manner.

JEANNE. You mean on account of the talk the waiters overheard—it means nothing to me, who has heard such things before when Maurice had had a few drinks. Then it is his custom to speculate on crimes and their punishment. Besides it seems to have been the woman in his company who dropped the most dangerous remarks. I should like to have a look into that woman's eyes.

ADOLPHE. My dear Jeanne, no matter how much harm that woman may have done you, she did nothing with evil intention—in fact, she had no intention whatever, but just followed the promptings of her nature. I know her to be a good soul and one who can very well bear being looked straight in the eye.

JEANNE. Your judgment in this matter, Adolphe, has great value to me, and I believe what you say. It means that I cannot hold anybody but myself responsible for what has happened. It is my carelessness that is now being punished. [She begins to cry.]

ABBÉ. Don't accuse yourself unjustly! I know you, and the serious spirit in which you have regarded your motherhood. That your assumption of this responsibility had not been sanctioned by religion and the civil law was not your fault. No, we are here facing something quite different.

ADOLPHE. What then?

ABBÉ. Who can tell?

(HENRIETTE enters, dressed in travelling suit.)

ADOLPHE. [Rises with an air of determination and goes to meet HENRIETTE] You here?

HENRIETTE. Yes, where is Maurice?

ADOLPHE. Do you know—or don't you?

HENRIETTE. I know everything. Excuse me, Madame Catherine, but I was ready to start and absolutely had to step in here a moment. [To ADOLPHE] Who is that woman?—Oh!

(HENRIETTE and JEANNE stare at each other.)

(EMILE appears in the kitchen door.)

HENRIETTE. [To JEANNE] I ought to say something, but it matters very little, for anything I can say must sound like an insult or a mockery. But if I ask you simply to believe that I share your deep sorrow as much as anybody standing closer to you, then you must not turn away from me. You mustn't, for I deserve your pity if not your forbearance. [Holds out her hand.]

JEANNE. [Looks hard at her] I believe you now—and in the next moment I don't. [Takes HENRIETTE'S hand.]

HENRIETTE. [Kisses JEANNE'S hand] Thank you!

JEANNE. [Drawing back her hand] Oh, don't! I don't deserve it! I don't deserve it!

ABBÉ. Pardon me, but while we are gathered here and peace seems to prevail temporarily at least, won't you, Mademoiselle Henriette, shed some light into all the uncertainty and darkness surrounding the main point of accusation? I ask you, as a friend among friends, to tell us what you meant with all that talk about killing, and crime, and the Place de Roquette. That your words had no connection with the death of the child, we have reason to believe, but it would give us added assurance to hear what you were really talking about. Won't you tell us?

HENRIETTE. [After a pause] That I cannot tell! No, I cannot!

ADOLPHE. Henriette, do tell! Give us the word that will relieve us all.

HENRIETTE. I cannot! Don't ask me!

ABBÉ. This is not the work of man!

HENRIETTE. Oh, that this moment had to come! And in this manner! [To JEANNE] Madame, I swear that I am not guilty of your child's death. Is that enough?

JEANNE. Enough for us, but not for Justice.

HENRIETTE. Justice! If you knew how true your words are!

ABBÉ. [To HENRIETTE] And if you knew what you were saying just now!

HENRIETTE. Do you know that better than I?

ABBÉ. Yes, I do.

(HENRIETTE looks fixedly at the ABBÉ.)

ABBÉ. Have no fear, for even if I guess your secret, it will not be exposed. Besides, I have nothing to do with human justice, but a great deal with divine mercy.

MAURICE. [Enters hastily, dressed for travelling. He doesn't look at the others, who are standing in the background, but goes straight up to the counter, where MME. CATHERINE is sitting.] You are not angry at me, Madame Catherine, because I didn't show up. I have come now to apologise to you before I start for the South at eight o'clock this evening.

(MME. CATHERINE is too startled to say a word.)

MAURICE. Then you are angry at me? [Looks around] What does all this mean? Is it a dream, or what is it? Of course, I can see that it is all real, but it looks like a wax cabinet—There is Jeanne, looking like a statue and dressed in black—And Henriette looking like a corpse—What does it mean?

(All remain silent.)

MAURICE. Nobody answers. It must mean something dreadful. [Silence] But speak, please! Adolphe, you are my friend, what is it? [Pointing to EMILE] And there is a detective!

ADOLPHE. [Comes forward] You don't know then?

MAURICE. Nothing at all. But I must know!

ADOLPHE. Well, then—Marion is dead.

MAURICE. Marion—dead?

ADOLPHE. Yes, she died this morning.

MAURICE. [To JEANNE] So that's why you are in mourning. Jeanne, Jeanne, who has done this to us?

JEANNE. He who holds life and death in his hand.

MAURICE. But I saw her looking well and happy this morning. How did it happen? Who did it? Somebody must have done it? [His eyes seek HENRIETTE.]

ADOLPHE. Don't look for the guilty one here, for there is none to he found. Unfortunately the police have turned their suspicion in a direction where none ought to exist.

MAURICE. What direction is that?

ADOLPHE. Well—you may as well know that, your reckless talk last night and this morning has placed you in a light that is anything but favourable.

MAURICE, So they were listening to us. Let me see, what were we saying— I remember!—Then I am lost!

ADOLPHE. But if you explain your thoughtless words we will believe you.

MAURICE. I cannot! And I will not! I shall be sent to prison, but it doesn't matter. Marion is dead! Dead! And I have killed her!

(General consternation.)

ADOLPHE. Think of what you are saying! Weigh your words! Do you realise what you said just now?

MAURICE. What did I say?

ADOLPHE. You said that you had killed Marion.

MAURICE. Is there a human being here who could believe me a murderer, and who could hold me capable of taking my own child's life? You who know me, Madame Catherine, tell me: do you believe, can you believe—

MME. CATHERINE. I don't know any longer what to believe. What the heart thinketh the tongue speaketh. And your tongue has spoken evil words.

MAURICE. She doesn't believe me!

ADOLPHE. But explain your words, man! Explain what you meant by saying that "your love would kill everything that stood in its way."

MAURICE. So they know that too—Are you willing to explain it, Henriette?

HENRIETTE. No, I cannot do that.

ABBÉ. There is something wrong behind all this and you have lost our sympathy, my friend. A while ago I could have sworn that you were innocent, and I wouldn't do that now.

MAURICE. [To JEANNE] What you have to say means more to me than anything else. JEANNE. [Coldly] Answer a question first: who was it you cursed during that orgie out there?

MAURICE. Have I done that too? Maybe. Yes, I am guilty, and yet I am guiltless. Let me go away from here, for I am ashamed of myself, and I have done more wrong than I can forgive myself.

HENRIETTE. [To ADOLPHE] Go with him and see that he doesn't do himself any harm.

ADOLPHE. Shall I—?

HENRIETTE. Who else?

ADOLPHE. [Without bitterness] You are nearest to it—Sh! A carriage is stopping outside.

MME. CATHERINE. It's the Commissaire. Well, much as I have seen of life, I could never have believed that success and fame were such short-lived things.

MAURICE. [To HENRIETTE] From the triumphal chariot to the patrol wagon!

JEANNE. [Simply] And the ass—who was that?

ADOLPHE. Oh, that must have been me.

COMMISSAIRE. [Enters with a paper in his hand] A summons to Police Headquarters—to-night, at once—for Monsieur Maurice Gérard—and for Mademoiselle Henrietta Mauclerc—both here?

MAURICE and HENRIETTE. Yes.

MAURICE. Is this an arrest?

COMMISSAIRE. Not yet. Only a summons.

MAURICE. And then?

COMMISSAIRE. We don't know yet.

(MAURICE and HENRIETTE go toward the door.)

MAURICE. Good-bye to all!

(Everybody shows emotion. The COMMISSAIRE, MAURICE, and HENRIETTE go out.)

EMILE. [Enters and goes up to JEANNE] Now I'll take you home, sister.

JEANNE. And what do you think of all this?

EMILE. The man is innocent.

ABBÉ. But as I see it, it is, and must always be, something despicable to break one's promise, and it becomes unpardonable when a woman and her child are involved.

EMILE. Well, I should rather feel that way, too, now when it concerns my own sister, but unfortunately I am prevented from throwing the first stone because I have done the same thing myself.

ABBÉ. Although I am free from blame in that respect, I am not throwing any stones either, but the act condemns itself and is punished by its consequences.

JEANNE. Pray for him! For both of them!

ABBÉ. No, I'll do nothing of the kind, for it is an impertinence to want to change the counsels of the Lord. And what has happened here is, indeed, not the work of man.

(Curtain.)

SECOND SCENE

(THe Auberge des Adrets. ADOLPHE and HENRIETTE are seated at the same table where MAURICE and HENRIETTE were sitting in the second act. A cup of coffee stands in front of ADOLPHE. HENRIETTE has ordered nothing.)

ADOLPHE. You believe then that he will come here?

HENRIETTE. I am sure. He was released this noon for lack of evidence, but he didn't want to show himself in the streets before it was dark.

ADOLPHE. Poor fellow! Oh, I tell you, life seems horrible to me since yesterday.

HENRIETTE. And what about me? I am afraid to live, dare hardly breathe, dare hardly think even, since I know that somebody is spying not only on my words but on my thoughts.

ADOLPHE. So it was here you sat that night when I couldn't find you?

HENRIETTE. Yes, but don't talk of it. I could die from shame when I think of it. Adolphe, you are made of a different, a better, stuff than he or I—

ADOLPHE. Sh, sh, sh!

HENRIETTE. Yes, indeed! And what was it that made me stay here? I was lazy; I was tired; his success intoxicated me and bewitched me—I cannot explain it. But if you had come, it would never have happened. And to-day you are great, and he is small—less than the least of all. Yesterday he had one hundred thousand francs. To-day he has nothing, because his play has been withdrawn. And public opinion will never excuse him, for his lack of faith will be judged as harshly as if he were the murderer, and those that see farthest hold that the child died from sorrow, so that he was responsible for it anyhow.

ADOLPHE. You know what my thoughts are in this matter, Henriette, but I should like to know that both of you are spotless. Won't you tell me what those dreadful words of yours meant? It cannot be a chance that your talk in a festive moment like that dealt so largely with killing and the scaffold.

HENRIETTE. It was no chance. It was something that had to be said, something I cannot tell you—probably because I have no right to appear spotless in your eyes, seeing that I am not spotless.

ADOLPHE. All this is beyond me.

HENRIETTE. Let us talk of something else—Do you believe there are many unpunished criminals at large among us, some of whom may even be our intimate friends?

ADOLPHE. [Nervously] Why? What do you mean?

HENRIETTE. Don't you believe that every human being at some time or another has been guilty of some kind of act which would fall under the law if it were discovered?

ADOLPHE. Yes, I believe that is true, but no evil act escapes being punished by one's own conscience at least. [Rises and unbuttons his coat] And—nobody is really good who has not erred. [Breathing heavily] For in order to know how to forgive, one must have been in need of forgiveness—I had a friend whom we used to regard as a model man. He never spoke a hard word to anybody; he forgave everything and everybody; and he suffered insults with a strange satisfaction that we couldn't explain. At last, late in life, he gave me his secret in a single word: I am a penitent! [He sits down again.]

(HENRIETTE remains silent, looking at him with surprise.)

ADOLPHE. [As if speaking to himself] There are crimes not mentioned in the Criminal Code, and these are the worse ones, for they have to be punished by ourselves, and no judge could be more severe than we are against our own selves.

HENRIETTE. [After a pause] Well, that friend of yours, did he find peace?

ADOLPHE. After endless self-torture he reached a certain degree of composure, but life had never any real pleasures to offer him. He never dared to accept any kind of distinction; he never dared to feel himself entitled to a kind word or even well-earned praise: in a word, he could never quite forgive himself.

HENRIETTE. Never? What had he done then?

ADOLPHE. He had wished the life out of his father. And when his father suddenly died, the son imagined himself to have killed him. Those imaginations were regarded as signs of some mental disease, and he was sent to an asylum. From this he was discharged after a time as wholly recovered—as they put it. But the sense of guilt remained with him, and so he continued to punish himself for his evil thoughts.

HENRIETTE. Are you sure the evil will cannot kill?

ADOLPHE. You mean in some mystic way?

HENRIETTE. As you please. Let it go at mystic. In my own family—I am sure that my mother and my sisters killed my father with their hatred. You see, he had the awful idea that he must oppose all our tastes and inclinations. Wherever he discovered a natural gift, he tried to root it out. In that way he aroused a resistance that accumulated until it became like an electrical battery charged with hatred. At last it grew so powerful that he languished away, became depolarised, lost his will-power, and, in the end, came to wish himself dead.

ADOLPHE. And your conscience never troubled you?

HENRIETTE. No, and furthermore, I don't know what conscience is.

ADOLPHE. You don't? Well, then you'll soon learn. [Pause] How do you believe Maurice will look when he gets here? What do you think he will say?

HENRIETTE. Yesterday morning, you know, he and I tried to make the same kind of guess about you while we were waiting for you.

ADOLPHE. Well?

HENRIETTE. We guessed entirely wrong.

ADOLPHE. Can you tell me why you sent for me?

HENRIETTE. Malice, arrogance, outright cruelty!

ADOLPHE. How strange it is that you can admit your faults and yet not repent of them.

HENRIETTE. It must be because I don't feel quite responsible for them. They are like the dirt left behind by things handled during the day and washed off at night. But tell me one thing: do you really think so highly of humanity as you profess to do?

ADOLPHE. Yes, we are a little better than our reputation—and a little worse.

HENRIETTE. That is not a straightforward answer.

ADOLPHE. No, it isn't. But are you willing to answer me frankly when I ask you: do you still love Maurice?

HENRIETTE. I cannot tell until I see him. But at this moment I feel no longing for him, and it seems as if I could very well live without him.

ADOLPHE. It's likely you could, but I fear you have become chained to his fate—Sh! Here he comes.

HENRIETTE. How everything repeats itself. The situation is the same, the very words are the same, as when we were expecting you yesterday.

MAURICE. [Enters, pale as death, hollow-eyed, unshaven] Here I am, my dear friends, if this be me. For that last night in a cell changed me into a new sort of being. [Notices HENRIETTE and ADOLPHE.]

ADOLPHE. Sit down and pull yourself together, and then we can talk things over.

MAURICE. [To HENRIETTE] Perhaps I am in the way?

ADOLPHE. Now, don't get bitter.

MAURICE. I have grown bad in these twenty-four hours, and suspicious also, so I guess I'll soon be left to myself. And who wants to keep company with a murderer?

HENRIETTE. But you have been cleared of the charge.

MAURICE. [Picks up a newspaper] By the police, yes, but not by public opinion. Here you see the murderer Maurice Gérard, once a playwright, and his mistress, Henriette Mauclerc—

HENRIETTE. O my mother and my sisters—my mother! Jesus have mercy!

MAURICE. And can you see that I actually look like a murderer? And then it is suggested that my play was stolen. So there isn't a vestige left of the victorious hero from yesterday. In place of my own, the name of Octave, my enemy, appears on the bill-boards, and he is going to collect my one hundred thousand francs. O Solon, Solon! Such is fortune, and such is fame! You are fortunate, Adolphe, because you have not yet succeeded.

HENRIETTE. So you don't know that Adolphe has made a great success in London and carried off the first prize?

MAURICE. [Darkly] No, I didn't know that. Is it true, Adolphe?

ADOLPHE. It is true, but I have returned the prize.

HENRIETTE. [With emphasis] That I didn't know! So you are also prevented from accepting any distinctions—like your friend?

ADOLPHE. My friend? [Embarrassed] Oh, yes, yes!

MAURICE. Your success gives me pleasure, but it puts us still farther apart.

ADOLPHE. That's what I expected, and I suppose I'll be as lonely with my success as you with your adversity. Think of it—that people feel hurt by your fortune! Oh, it's ghastly to be alive!

MAURICE. You say that! What am I then to say? It is as if my eyes had been covered with a black veil, and as if the colour and shape of all life had been changed by it. This room looks like the room I saw yesterday, and yet it is quite different. I recognise both of you, of course, but your faces are new to me. I sit here and search for words because I don't know what to say to you. I ought to defend myself, but I cannot. And I almost miss the cell, for it protected me, at least, against the curious glances that pass right through me. The murderer Maurice and his mistress! You don't love me any longer, Henriette, and no more do I care for you. To-day you are ugly, clumsy, insipid, repulsive.

(Two men in civilian clothes have quietly seated themselves at a table in the background.)

ADOLPHE. Wait a little and get your thoughts together. That you have been discharged and cleared of all suspicion must appear in some of the evening papers. And that puts an end to the whole matter. Your play will be put on again, and if it comes to the worst, you can write a new one. Leave Paris for a year and let everything become forgotten. You who have exonerated mankind will be exonerated yourself.

MAURICE. Ha-ha! Mankind! Ha-ha!

ADOLPHE. You have ceased to believe in goodness? MAURICE. Yes, if I ever did believe in it. Perhaps it was only a mood, a manner of looking at things, a way of being polite to the wild beasts. When I, who was held among the best, can be so rotten to the core, what must then be the wretchedness of the rest?

ADOLPHE. Now I'll go out and get all the evening papers, and then we'll undoubtedly have reason to look at things in a different way.

MAURICE. [Turning toward the background] Two detectives!—It means that I am released under surveillance, so that I can give myself away by careless talking.

ADOLPHE. Those are not detectives. That's only your imagination. I recognise both of them. [Goes toward the door.]

MAURICE. Don't leave us alone, Adolphe. I fear that Henriette and I may come to open explanations.

ADOLPHE. Oh, be sensible, Maurice, and think of your future. Try to keep him quiet, Henriette. I'll be back in a moment. [Goes out.]

HENRIETTE. Well, Maurice, what do you think now of our guilt or guiltlessness?

MAURICE. I have killed nobody. All I did was to talk a lot of nonsense while I was drunk. But it is your crime that comes back, and that crime you have grafted on to me.

HENRIETTE. Oh, that's the tone you talk in now!—Was it not you who cursed your own child, and wished the life out of it, and wanted to go away without saying good-bye to anybody? And was it not I who made you visit Marion and show yourself to Madame Catherine?

MAURICE. Yes, you are right. Forgive me! You proved yourself more human than I, and the guilt is wholly my own. Forgive me! But all the same I am without guilt. Who has tied this net from which I can never free myself? Guilty and guiltless; guiltless and yet guilty! Oh, it is driving me mad—Look, now they sit over there and listen to us—And no waiter comes to take our order. I'll go out and order a cup of tea. Do you want anything?

HENRIETTE. Nothing.

(MAURICE goes out.)

FIRST DETECTIVE. [Goes up to HENRIETTE] Let me look at your papers.

HENRIETTE. How dare you speak to me?

DETECTIVE. Dare? I'll show you!

HENRIETTE. What do you mean?

DETECTIVE. It's my job to keep an eye on street-walkers. Yesterday you came here with one man, and today with another. That's as good as walking the streets. And unescorted ladies don't get anything here. So you'd better get out and come along with me.

HENRIETTE. My escort will be back in a moment.

DETECTIVE. Yes, and a pretty kind of escort you've got—the kind that doesn't help a girl a bit!

HENRIETTE. O God! My mother, my sisters!—I am of good family, I tell you.

DETECTIVE. Yes, first-rate family, I am sure. But you are too well known through the papers. Come along!

HENRIETTE. Where? What do you mean?

DETECTIVE. Oh, to the Bureau, of course. There you'll get a nice little card and a license that brings you free medical care.

HENRIETTE. O Lord Jesus, you don't mean it!

DETECTIVE. [Grabbing HENRIETTE by the arm] Don't I mean it?

HENRIETTE. [Falling on her knees] Save me, Maurice! Help!

DETECTIVE. Shut up, you fool!

(MAURICE enters, followed by WAITER.)

WAITER. Gentlemen of that kind are not served here. You just pay and get out! And take the girl along!

MAURICE. [Crushed, searches his pocket-book for money] Henriette, pay for me, and let us get away from this place. I haven't a sou left.

WAITER. So the lady has to put up for her Alphonse! Alphonse! Do you know what that is?

HENRIETTE. [Looking through her pocket-book] Oh, merciful heavens! I have no money either!—Why doesn't Adolphe come back?

DETECTIVE. Well, did you ever see such rotters! Get out of here, and put up something as security. That kind of ladies generally have their fingers full of rings.

MAURICE. Can it be possible that we have sunk so low?

HENRIETTE. [Takes off a ring and hands it to the WAITER] The Abbé was right: this is not the work of man.

MAURICE. No, it's the devil's!—But if we leave before Adolphe returns, he will think that we have deceived him and run away.

HENRIETTE. That would be in keeping with the rest—But we'll go into the river now, won't we?

MAURICE. [Takes HENRIETTE by the hand as they walk out together] Into the river—yes!

(Curtain.)

ACT IV

FIRST SCENE
 (IN the Luxembourg Gardens, at the group of Adam and Eve. The wind is shaking the trees and stirring up dead leaves, straws, and pieces of paper from the ground.)

(MAURICE and HENRIETTE are seated on a bench.)

HENRIETTE. So you don't want to die?

MAURICE. No, I am afraid. I imagine that I am going to be very cold down there in the grave, with only a sheet to cover me and a few shavings to lie on. And besides that, it seems to me as if there were still some task waiting for me, but I cannot make out what it is.

HENRIETTE. But I can guess what it is.

MAURICE. Tell me.

HENRIETTE. It is revenge. You, like me, must have suspected Jeanne and Emile of sending the detectives after me yesterday. Such a revenge on a rival none but a woman could devise.

MAURICE. Exactly what I was thinking. But let me tell you that my suspicions go even further. It seems as if my sufferings during these last few days had sharpened my wits. Can you explain, for instance, why the waiter from the Auberge des Adrets and the head waiter from the Pavilion were not called to testify at the hearing?

HENRIETTE. I never thought of it before. But now I know why. They had nothing to tell, because they had not been listening.

MAURICE. But how could the Commissaire then know what we had been saying?

HENRIETTE. He didn't know, but he figured it out. He was guessing, and he guessed right. Perhaps he had had to deal with some similar case before.

MAURICE. Or else he concluded from our looks what we had been saying. There are those who can read other people's thoughts— Adolphe being the dupe, it seemed quite natural that we should have called him an ass. It's the rule, I understand, although it's varied at times by the use of "idiot" instead. But ass was nearer at hand in this case, as we had been talking of carriages and triumphal chariots. It is quite simple to figure out a fourth fact, when you have three known ones to start from.

HENRIETTE. Just think that we have let ourselves be taken in so completely.

MAURICE. That's the result of thinking too well of one's fellow beings. This is all you get out of it. But do you know, I suspect somebody else back of the Commissaire, who, by-the-bye, must be a full-fledged scoundrel.

HENRIETTE. You mean the Abbé, who was taking the part of a private detective.

MAURICE. That's what I mean. That man has to receive all kinds of confessions. And note you: Adolphe himself told us he had been at the Church of St. Germain that morning. What was he doing there? He was blabbing, of course, and bewailing his fate. And then the priest put the questions together for the Commissaire.

HENRIETTE. Tell me something: do you trust Adolphe?

MAURICE. I trust no human being any longer.

HENRIETTE. Not even Adolphe?

MAURICE. Him least of all. How could I trust an enemy—a man from whom I have taken away his mistress?

HENRIETTE. Well, as you were the first one to speak of this, I'll give you some data about our friend. You heard he had returned that medal from London. Do you know his reason for doing so?

MAURICE. No.

HENRIETTE. He thinks himself unworthy of it, and he has taken a penitential vow never to receive any kind of distinction.

MAURICE. Can that he possible? But what has he done?

HENRIETTE. He has committed a crime of the kind that is not punishable under the law. That's what he gave me to understand indirectly.

MAURICE. He, too! He, the best one of all, the model man, who never speaks a hard word of anybody and who forgives everything.

HENRIETTE. Well, there you can see that we are no worse than others. And yet we are being hounded day and night as if devils were after us.

MAURICE. He, also! Then mankind has not been slandered—But if he has been capable of *one* crime, then you may expect anything of him. Perhaps it was he who sent the police after you yesterday. Coming to think of it now, it was he who sneaked away from us when he saw that we were in the papers, and he lied when he insisted that those fellows were not detectives. But, of course, you may expect anything from a deceived lover.

HENRIETTE. Could he be as mean as that? No, it is impossible, impossible!

MAURICE. Why so? If he is a scoundrel?—What were you two talking of yesterday, before I came?

HENRIETTE. He had nothing but good to say of you.

MAURICE. That's a lie!

HENRIETTE. [Controlling herself and changing her tone] Listen. There is one person on whom you have cast no suspicion whatever— for what reason, I don't know. Have you thought of Madame Catherine's wavering attitude in this matter? Didn't she say finally that she believed you capable of anything?

MAURICE. Yes, she did, and that shows what kind of person she is. To think evil of other people without reason, you must be a villain yourself.

(HENRIETTE looks hard at him. Pause.)

HENRIETTE. To think evil of others, you must be a villain yourself.

MAURICE. What do you mean?

HENRIETTE. What I said.

MAURICE. Do you mean that I—?

HENRIETTE. Yes, that's what I mean now! Look here! Did you meet anybody but Marion when you called there yesterday morning?

MAURICE. Why do you ask?

HENRIETTE. Guess!

MAURICE. Well, as you seem to know—I met Jeanne, too.

HENRIETTE. Why did you lie to me?

MAURICE. I wanted to spare you.

HENRIETTE. And now you want me to believe in one who has been lying to me? No, my boy, now I believe you guilty of that murder.

MAURICE. Wait a moment! We have now reached the place for which my thoughts have been heading all the time, though I resisted as long as possible. It's queer that what lies next to one is seen last of all, and what one doesn't *want* to believe cannot be believed—Tell me something: where did you go yesterday morning, after we parted in the Bois?

HENRIETTE. [Alarmed] Why?

MAURICE. You went either to Adolphe—which you couldn't do, as he was attending a lesson—or you went to—Marion!

HENRIETTE. Now I am convinced that you are the murderer.

MAURICE. And I, that you are the murderess! You alone had an interest in getting the child out of the way—to get rid of the rock on the road, as you so aptly put it.

HENRIETTE. It was you who said that.

MAURICE. And the one who had an interest in it must have committed the crime.

HENRIETTE. Now, Maurice, we have been running around and around in this tread-mill, scourging each other. Let us quit before we get to the point of sheer madness.

MAURICE. You have reached that point already.

HENRIETTE. Don't you think it's time for us to part, before we drive each other insane?

MAURICE. Yes, I think so.

HENRIETTE. [Rising] Good-bye then!

(Two men in civilian clothes become visible in the background.)

HENRIETTE. [Turns and comes back to MAURICE] There they are again!

MAURICE. The dark angels that want to drive us out of the garden.

HENRIETTE. And force us back upon each other as if we were chained together.

MAURICE. Or as if we were condemned to lifelong marriage. Are we really to marry? To settle down in the same place? To be able to close the door behind us and perhaps get peace at last?

HENRIETTE. And shut ourselves up in order to torture each other to death; get behind locks and bolts, with a ghost for marriage portion; you torturing me with the memory of Adolphe, and I getting back at you with Jeanne—and Marion.

MAURICE. Never mention the name of Marion again! Don't you know that she was to be buried today—at this very moment perhaps?

HENRIETTE. And you are not there? What does that mean?

MAURICE. It means that both Jeanne and the police have warned me against the rage of the people.

HENRIETTE. A coward, too?

MAURICE. All the vices! How could you ever have cared for me?

HENRIETTE. Because two days ago you were another person, well worthy of being loved—

MAURICE. And now sunk to such a depth!

HENRIETTE. It isn't that. But you are beginning to flaunt bad qualities which are not your own.

MAURICE. But yours?

HENRIETTE. Perhaps, for when you appear a little worse I feel myself at once a little better.

MAURICE. It's like passing on a disease to save one's self- respect.

HENRIETTE. And how vulgar you have become, too!

MAURICE. Yes, I notice it myself, and I hardly recognise myself since that night in the cell. They put in one person and let out another through that gate which separates us from the rest of society. And now I feel myself the enemy of all mankind: I should like to set fire to the earth and dry up the oceans, for nothing less than a universal conflagration can wipe out my dishonour.

HENRIETTE. I had a letter from my mother today. She is the widow of a major in the army, well educated, with old-fashioned ideas of honour and that kind of thing. Do you want to read the letter? No, you don't!—Do you know that I am an outcast? My respectable acquaintances will have nothing to do with me, and if I show myself on the streets alone the police will take me. Do you realise now that we have to get married?

MAURICE. We despise each other, and yet we have to marry: that is hell pure and simple! But, Henriette, before we unite our destinies you must tell me your secret, so that we may be on more equal terms.

HENRIETTE. All right, I'll tell you. I had a friend who got into trouble— you understand. I wanted to help her, as her whole future was at stake—and she died!

MAURICE. That was reckless, but one might almost call it noble, too.

HENRIETTE. You say so now, but the next time you lose your temper you will accuse me of it.

MAURICE. No, I won't. But I cannot deny that it has shaken my faith in you and that it makes me afraid of you. Tell me, is her lover still alive, and does he know to what extent you were responsible?

HENRIETTE. He was as guilty as I.

MAURICE. And if his conscience should begin to trouble him—such things do happen—and if he should feel inclined to confess: then you would be lost.

HENRIETTE. I know it, and it is this constant dread which has made me rush from one dissipation to another—so that I should never have time to wake up to full consciousness.

MAURICE. And now you want me to take my marriage portion out of your dread. That's asking a little too much.

HENRIETTE. But when I shared the shame of Maurice the murderer—

MAURICE. Oh, let's come to an end with it!

HENRIETTE. No, the end is not yet, and I'll not let go my hold until I have put you where you belong. For you can't go around thinking yourself better than I am.

MAURICE. So you want to fight me then? All right, as you please!

HENRIETTE. A fight on life and death!

(The rolling of drums is heard in the distance.)

MAURICE. The garden is to be closed. "Cursed is the ground for thy sake; thorns and thistles shall it bring forth to thee."

HENRIETTE. "And the Lord God said unto the woman—"

A GUARD. [In uniform, speaking very politely] Sorry, but the garden has to be closed.

(Curtain.)

SECOND SCENE

(THE Crêmerie. MME. CATHERINE is sitting at the counter making entries into an account book. ADOLPHE and HENRIETTE are seated at a table.)

ADOLPHE. [Calmly and kindly] But if I give you my final assurance that I didn't run away, but that, on the contrary, I thought you had played me false, this ought to convince you.

HENRIETTE. But why did you fool us by saying that those fellows were not policemen?

ADOLPHE. I didn't think myself that they were, and then I wanted to reassure you.

HENRIETTE. When you say it, I believe you. But then you must also believe me, if I reveal my innermost thoughts to you.

ADOLPHE. Go on.

HENRIETTE. But you mustn't come back with your usual talk of fancies and delusions.

ADOLPHE. You seem to have reason to fear that I may.

HENRIETTE. I fear nothing, but I know you and your scepticism— Well, and then you mustn't tell this to anybody—promise me!

ADOLPHE. I promise.

HENRIETTE. Now think of it, although I must say it's something terrible: I have partial evidence that Maurice is guilty, or at least, I have reasonable suspicions—

ADOLPHE. You don't mean it!

HENRIETTE. Listen, and judge for yourself. When Maurice left me in the Bois, he said he was going to see Marion alone, as the mother was out. And now I have discovered afterward that he did meet the mother. So that he has been lying to me.

ADOLPHE. That's possible, and his motive for doing so may have been the best, but how can anybody conclude from it that he is guilty of a murder?

HENRIETTE. Can't you see that?—Don't you understand?

ADOLPHE. Not at all.

HENRIETTE. Because you don't want to!—Then there is nothing left for me but to report him, and we'll see whether he can prove an alibi.

ADOLPHE. Henriette, let me tell you the grim truth. You, like he, have reached the border line of—insanity. The demons of distrust have got hold of you, and each of you is using his own sense of partial guilt to wound the other with. Let me see if I can make a straight guess: he has also come to suspect you of killing his child?

HENRIETTE. Yes, he's mad enough to do so.

ADOLPHE. You call his suspicions mad, but not your own.

HENRIETTE. You have first to prove the contrary, or that I suspect him unjustly.

ADOLPHE. Yes, that's easy. A new autopsy has proved that Marion died of a well-known disease, the queer name of which I cannot recall just now.

HENRIETTE. Is it true?

ADOLPHE. The official report is printed in today's paper.

HENRIETTE. I don't take any stock in it. They can make up that kind of thing.

ADOLPHE. Beware, Henriette—or you may, without knowing it, pass across that border line. Beware especially of throwing out accusations that may put you into prison. Beware! [He places his hand on her head] You hate Maurice?

HENRIETTE. Beyond all bounds!

ADOLPHE. When love turns into hatred, it means that it was tainted from the start.

HENRIETTE. [In a quieter mood] What am I to do? Tell me, you who are the only one that understands me.

ADOLPHE. But you don't want any sermons.

HENRIETTE. Have you nothing else to offer me?

ADOLPHE. Nothing else. But they have helped me.

HENRIETTE. Preach away then!

ADOLPHE. Try to turn your hatred against yourself. Put the knife to the evil spot in yourself, for it is there that *your* trouble roots.

HENRIETTE. Explain yourself.

ADOLPHE. Part from Maurice first of all, so that you cannot nurse your qualms of conscience together. Break off your career as an artist, for the only thing that led you into it was a craving for freedom and fun—as they call it. And you have seen now how much fun there is in it. Then go home to your mother.

HENRIETTE. Never!

ADOLPHE. Some other place then.

HENRIETTE. I suppose you know, Adolphe, that I have guessed your secret and why you wouldn't accept the prize?

ADOLPHE. Oh, I assumed that you would understand a half-told story.

HENRIETTE. Well—what did you do to get peace?

ADOLPHE. What I have suggested: I became conscious of my guilt, repented, decided to turn over a new leaf, and arranged my life like that of a penitent.

HENRIETTE. How can you repent when, like me, you have no conscience? Is repentance an act of grace bestowed on you as faith is?

ADOLPHE. Everything is a grace, but it isn't granted unless you seek it— Seek!

(HENRIETTE remains silent.)

ADOLPHE. But don't wait beyond the allotted time, or you may harden yourself until you tumble down into the irretrievable.

HENRIETTE. [After a pause] Is conscience fear of punishment?

ADOLPHE. No, it is the horror inspired in our better selves by the misdeeds of our lower selves.

HENRIETTE. Then I must have a conscience also?

ADOLPHE. Of course you have, but—

HENRIETTE, Tell me, Adolphe, are you what they call religious?

ADOLPHE. Not the least bit.

HENRIETTE. It's all so queer—What is religion?

ADOLPHE. Frankly speaking, I don't know! And I don't think anybody else can tell you. Sometimes it appears to me like a punishment, for nobody becomes religious without having a bad conscience.

HENRIETTE. Yes, it is a punishment. Now I know what to do. Good-bye, Adolphe!

ADOLPHE. You'll go away from here?

HENRIETTE. Yes, I am going—to where you said. Good-bye my friend! Good-bye, Madame Catherine!

MME. CATHERINE. Have you to go in such a hurry?

HENRIETTE. Yes.

ADOLPHE. Do you want me to go with you?

HENRIETTE. No, it wouldn't do. I am going alone, alone as I came here, one day in Spring, thinking that I belonged where I don't belong, and believing there was something called freedom, which does not exist. Good-bye! [Goes out.]

MME. CATHERINE. I hope that lady never comes back, and I wish she had never come here at all!

ADOLPHE. Who knows but that she may have had some mission to fill here? And at any rate she deserves pity, endless pity.

MME. CATHERINE. I don't, deny it, for all of us deserve that.

ADOLPHE. And she has even done less wrong than the rest of us.

MME. CATHERINE. That's possible, but not probable.

ADOLPHE. You are always so severe, Madame Catherine. Tell me: have you never done anything wrong?

MME. CATHERINE. [Startled] Of course, as I am a sinful human creature. But if you have been on thin ice and fallen in, you have a right to tell others to keep away. And you may do so without being held severe or uncharitable. Didn't

I say to Monsieur Maurice the moment that lady entered here: Look out! Keep away! And he didn't, and so he fell in. Just like a naughty, self-willed child. And when a man acts like that he has to have a spanking, like any disobedient youngster.

ADOLPHE. Well, hasn't he had his spanking?

MME. CATHERINE. Yes, but it does not seem to have been enough, as he is still going around complaining.

ADOLPHE. That's a very popular interpretation of the whole intricate question.

MME. CATHERINE. Oh, pish! You do nothing but philosophise about your vices, and while you are still at it the police come along and solve the riddle. Now please leave me alone with my accounts!

ADOLPHE. There's Maurice now.

MME. CATHERINE. Yes, God bless him!

MAURICE. [Enters, his face very flushed, and takes a seat near ADOLPHE] Good evening.

(MME. CATHERINE nods and goes on figuring.)

ADOLPHE. Well, how's everything with you?

MAURICE. Oh, beginning to clear up.

ADOLPHE. [Hands him a newspaper, which MAURICE does not take] So you have read the paper?

MAURICE. No, I don't read the papers any longer. There's nothing but infamies in them.

ADOLPHE. But you had better read it first—

MAURICE. No, I won't! It's nothing but lies—But listen: I have found a new clue. Can you guess who committed that murder?

ADOLPHE. Nobody, nobody!

MAURICE. Do you know where Henriette was during that quarter hour when the child was left alone?—She was *there*! And it is she who has done it!

ADOLPHE. You are crazy, man.

MAURICE. Not I, but Henriette, is crazy. She suspects me and has threatened to report me.

ADOLPHE. Henriette was here a while ago, and she used the self- same words as you. Both of you are crazy, for it has been proved by a second autopsy that the child died from a well-known disease, the name of which I have forgotten.

MAURICE. It isn't true!

ADOLPHE. That's what she said also. But the official report is printed in the paper.

MAURICE. A report? Then they have made it up!

ADOLPHE. And that's also what she said. The two of you are suffering from the same mental trouble. But with her I got far enough to make her realise her own condition.

MAURICE. Where did she go?

ADOLPHE. She went far away from here to begin a new life.

MAURICE. Hm, hm!—Did you go to the funeral?

ADOLPHE. I did.

MAURICE. Well?

ADOLPHE. Well, Jeanne seemed resigned and didn't have a hard word to say about you.

MAURICE. She is a good woman.

ADOLPHE. Why did you desert her then?

MAURICE. Because I *was* crazy—blown up with pride especially—and then we had been drinking champagne—

ADOLPHE. Can you understand now why Jeanne wept when you drank champagne?

MAURICE. Yes, I understand now—And for that reason I have already written to her and asked her to forgive me—Do you think she will forgive me?

ADOLPHE. I think so, for it's not like her to hate anybody.

MAURICE. Do you think she will forgive me completely, so that she will come back to me?

ADOLPHE. Well, I don't know about *that*. You have shown yourself so poor in keeping faith that it is doubtful whether she will trust her fate to you any longer.

MAURICE. But I can feel that her fondness for me has not ceased, and I know she will come back to me.

ADOLPHE. How can you know that? How can you believe it? Didn't you even suspect her and that decent brother of hers of having sent the police after Henriette out of revenge?

MAURICE. But I don't believe it any longer—that is to say, I guess that fellow Emile is a pretty slick customer.

MME. CATHERINE. Now look here! What are you saying of Monsieur Emile? Of course, he is nothing but a workman, but if everybody kept as straight as he—There is no flaw in him, but a lot of sense and tact.

EMILE. [Enters] Monsieur Gérard?

MAURICE. That's me.

EMILE. Pardon me, but I have something to say to you in private.

MAURICE. Go right on. We are all friends here.

(The ABBÉ enters and sits down.)

EMILE. [With a glance at the ABBÉ] Perhaps after—

MAURICE. Never mind. The Abbé is also a friend, although he and I differ.

EMILE. You know who I am, Monsieur Gérard? My sister has asked me to give you this package as an answer to your letter.

(MAURICE takes the package and opens it.)

EMILE. And now I have only to add, seeing as I am in a way my sister's guardian, that, on her behalf as well as my own, I acknowledge you free of all obligations, now when the natural tie between you does not exist any longer.

MAURICE. But you must have a grudge against me?

EMILE. Must I? I can't see why. On the other hand, I should like to have a declaration from you, here in the presence of your friends, that you don't think either me or my sister capable of such a meanness as to send the police after Mademoiselle Henriette.

MAURICE. I wish to take back what I said, and I offer you my apology, if you will accept it.

EMILE. It is accepted. And I wish all of you a good evening. [Goes out.]

EVERYBODY. Good evening!

MAURICE. The tie and the gloves which Jeanne gave me for the opening night of my play, and which I let Henrietta throw into the fireplace. Who can have picked them up? Everything is dug up; everything comes back!—And when she gave them to me in the cemetery, she said she wanted me to look fine and handsome, so that other people would like me also—And she herself stayed at home—This hurt her too deeply, and well it might. I have no right to keep company with decent human beings. Oh, have I done this? Scoffed at a gift coming from a good heart; scorned a sacrifice offered to my own welfare. This was what I threw away in order to get—a laurel that is lying on the rubbish heap, and a bust that would have belonged in the pillory—Abbé, now I come over to you.

ABBÉ. Welcome!

MAURICE. Give me the word that I need.

ABBÉ. Do you expect me to contradict your self-accusations and inform you that you have done nothing wrong?

MAURICE. Speak the right word!

ABBÉ. With your leave, I'll say then that I have found your behaviour just as abominable as you have found it yourself.

MAURICE. What can I do, what can I do, to get out of this?

ABBÉ. You know as well as I do.

MAURICE. No, I know only that I am lost, that my life is spoiled, my career cut off, my reputation in this world ruined forever.

ABBÉ. And so you are looking for a new existence in some better world, which you are now beginning to believe in?

MAURICE. Yes, that's it.

ABBÉ. You have been living in the flesh and you want now to live in the spirit. Are you then so sure that this world has no more attractions for you?

MAURICE. None whatever! Honour is a phantom; gold, nothing but dry leaves; women, mere intoxicants. Let me hide myself behind your consecrated walls and forget this horrible dream that has filled two days and lasted two eternities.

ABBÉ. All right! But this is not the place to go into the matter more closely. Let us make an appointment for this evening at nine o'clock in the Church of St. Germain. For I am going to preach to the inmates of St. Lazare, and that may be your first step along the hard road of penitence.

MAURICE. Penitence?

ABBÉ. Well, didn't you wish—

MAURICE. Yes, yes!

ABBÉ. Then we have vigils between midnight and two o'clock.

MAURICE. That will be splendid!

ABBÉ. Give me your hand that you will not look back.

MAURICE. [Rising, holds out his hand] Here is my hand, and my will goes with it.

SERVANT GIRL. [Enters from the kitchen] A telephone call for Monsieur Maurice.

MAURICE. From whom?

SERVANT GIRL. From the theatre.

(MAURICE tries to get away, but the ABBÉ holds on to his hand.)

ABBÉ. [To the SERVANT GIRL] Find out what it is.

SERVANT GIRL. They want to know if Monsieur Maurice is going to attend the performance tonight.

ABBÉ. [To MAURICE, who is trying to get away] No, I won't let you go.

MAURICE. What performance is that?

ADOLPHE. Why don't you read the paper?

MME. CATHERINE and the ABBÉ. He hasn't read the paper?

MAURICE. It's all lies and slander. [To the SERVANT GIRL] Tell them that I am engaged for this evening: I am going to church.

(The SERVANT GIRL goes out into the kitchen.)

ADOLPHE. As you don't want to read the paper, I shall have to tell you that your play has been put on again, now when you are exonerated. And your literary friends have planned a demonstration for this evening in recognition of your indisputable talent.

MAURICE. It isn't true.

EVERYBODY. It is true.

MAURICE. [After a pause] I have not deserved it!

ABBÉ. Good!

ADOLPHE. And furthermore, Maurice—

MAURICE. [Hiding his face in his hands] Furthermore!

MME. CATHERINE. One hundred thousand francs! Do you see now that they come back to you? And the villa outside the city. Everything is coming back except Mademoiselle Henriette.

ABBÉ. [Smiling] You ought to take this matter a little more seriously, Madame Catherine.

MME. CATHERINE. Oh, I cannot—I just can't keep serious any longer!

[She breaks into open laughter, which she vainly tries to smother with her handkerchief.]

ADOLPHE. Say, Maurice, the play begins at eight.

ABBÉ. But the church services are at nine.

ADOLPHE. Maurice!

MME. CATHERINE. Let us hear what the end is going to be, Monsieur Maurice.

(MAURICE drops his head on the table, in his arms.)

ADOLPHE. Loose him, Abbé!

ABBÉ. No, it is not for me to loose or bind. He must do that himself.

MAURICE. [Rising] Well, I go with the Abbé.

ABBÉ. No, my young friend. I have nothing to give you but a scolding, which you can give yourself. And you owe a duty to yourself and to your good name. That you have got through with this as quickly as you have is to me a sign that you have suffered your punishment as intensely as if it had lasted an eternity. And when Providence absolves you there is nothing for me to add.

MAURICE. But why did the punishment have to be so hard when I was innocent?

ABBÉ. Hard? Only two days! And you were not innocent. For we have to stand responsible for our thoughts and words and desires also. And in your thought you became a murderer when your evil self wished the life out of your child.

MAURICE. You are right. But my decision is made. To-night I will meet you at the church in order to have a reckoning with myself— but to-morrow evening I go to the theatre.

MME. CATHERINE. A good solution, Monsieur Maurice.

ADOLPHE. Yes, that is the solution. Whew!

ABBÉ. Yes, so it is!

(Curtain.)

MISS JULIA

INTRODUCTION

THE volume containing the translation of "There Are Crimes and Crimes" had barely reached the public when word came across the ocean that August Strindberg had ended his long fight with life. His family had long suspected some serious organic trouble. Early in the year, when lie had just recovered from an illness of temporary character, their worst fears became confirmed. An examination disclosed a case of cancer in the stomach, and the disease progressed so rapidly that soon all hope of recovery was out of the question. On May 14, 1912, Strindberg died.

With his death peace came in more senses than one. All the fear and hatred which he had incurred by what was best as well as worst in him seemed to be laid at rest with his own worn-out body. The love and the admiration which he had son in far greater measure were granted unchecked expression. His burial, otherwise as simple as he himself had prescribed, was a truly national event. At the grave of the arch-rebel appeared a royal prince as official representative of the reigning house, the entire cabinet, and numerous members of the Riksdag. Thousands of men and women representing the best of Sweden's intellectual and artistic life went to the cemetery, though the hour of the funeral was eight o'clock in the morning. It was an event in which the masses and the classes shared a common sorrow, the standards of student organizations mingling with the banners of labour unions. And not only the capital, but the whole country, observed the day as one of mourning.

A thought frequently recurring in the comment passed on Strindberg's death by the European press was that, in some mysterious manner, he, more than any other writer, appeared to be the incarnation of the past century, with its nervous striving after truth, its fear of being duped, and its fretting dread that evolution and progress might prove antagonistic terms. And at that simple grave in Stockholm more than one bareheaded spectator must have heard the gravel rattle on the coffin-lid with a feeling that not only a great individual, but a whole human period—great in spite of all its weaknesses—was being laid away for ever.

Among more than half a hundred plays produced by Strindberg during his lifetime, none has won such widespread attention as "Miss Julia," both on account of its masterful construction and its gripping theme. Whether liking or disliking it, critics have repeatedly compared it with Ibsen's "Ghosts," and not always to the advantage of the latter work. It represents, first of all, its author's most determined and most daring endeavour to win the modern stage for Naturalism. If he failed in this effort, it must be recalled to his honour that he was among the first to proclaim his own failure and to advocate the seeking of new paths. When the work was still hot from his hands, however, he believed in it with all the fervour of which his spirit was capable, and to bring home its lesson the more forcibly, he added a preface, a sort of dramatic creed, explaining just what he had tried to do, and why. This preface, which has become hardly less famous than the play itself, is here, as I believe, for the first time rendered into English. The acuteness and exhaustiveness of its analysis serves not only to make it a psychological document of rare value, but also to save me much of the comment which without it might be deemed needful.

Years later, while engaged in conducting a theatre for the exclusive performance of his own plays at Stockholm, Strindberg formulated a new dramatic creed—that of his mystical period, in which he was wont to sign himself "the author of 'Gustavus Vasa,' 'The Dream Play,' 'The Last Knight,' etc." It took the form of a pamphlet entitled "A Memorandum to the Members of the Intimate Theatre from the Stage Director" (Stockholm, 1908). There he gave the following data concerning "Miss Julia," and the movement which that play helped to start:

"In the '80's the new time began to extend its demands for reform to the stage also. Zola declared war against the French comedy, with its Brussels carpets, its patent-leather shoes and patent-leather themes, and its dialogue reminding one of the questions and answers of the Catechism. In 1887 Antoine opened his Théâtre Libre at Paris, and 'Thérèse Raquin,' although nothing but an adapted novel, became the dominant model. It was the powerful theme and the concentrated form that showed innovation, although the unity of time was not yet observed, and curtain falls were retained. It was then I wrote my dramas: 'Miss Julia,' 'The Father,' and 'Creditors.'

"'Miss Julia,' which was equipped with a now well-known preface, was staged by Antoine, but not until 1892 or 1893, having previously been played by the Students' Association of the Copenhagen University in 1888 or 1889. In the spring of 1893 'Creditors' was put on at the Théâtre L'OEuvre, in Paris, and in the fall of the same year 'The Father' was given at the same theatre, with Philippe Garnier in the title part.

"But as early as 1889 the Freie Bühne had been started at Berlin, and before 1893 all three of my dramas had been performed. 'Miss Julia' was preceded by a lecture given by Paul Schlenther, now director of the Hofburg Theater at Vienna. The principal parts were played by Rosa Bertens, Emanuel Reicher, Rittner and Jarno. And Sigismund Lautenburg, director of the Residenz Theater, gave more than one hundred performances of 'Creditors.'

"Then followed a period of comparative silence, and the drama sank back into the old ruts, until, with the beginning of the new century, Reinhardt opened his Kleines Theater. There I was played from the start, being represented by the long one-act drama 'The Link,' as well as by 'Miss Julia' (with Eysoldt in the title part), and 'There Are Crimes and Crimes.'"

He went on to tell how one European city after another had got its "Little," or "Free," or "Intimate" theatre. And had he known of it, he might have added that the promising venture started by Mr. Winthrop Ames at New York comes as near as any one of its earlier rivals in the faithful embodiment of those theories which, with Promethean rashness, he had flung at the head of a startled world in 1888. For the usual thing has happened: what a quarter-century ago seemed almost ludicrous in its radicalism belongs to-day to the established traditions of every progressive stage.

Had Strindberg been content with his position of 1888, many honours now withheld might have fallen to his share. But like Ibsen, he was first and last— and to the very last!—an innovator, a leader of human thought and human endeavour. And so it happened that when the rest thought to have overtaken him, he had already hurried on to a more advanced position, heedless of the scorn poured on him by those to whom "consistency" is the foremost of all human virtues. Three years before his death we find him writing as follows in another pamphlet "An Open Letter to the Intimate Theatre," Stockholm, 1909—of the position once assumed so proudly and so confidently by himself:

"As the Intimate Theatre counts its inception from the successful performance of 'Miss Julia' in 1900, it was quite natural that the young director (August Falck) should feel the influence of the Preface, which recommended a search for actuality. But that was twenty years ago, and although I do not feel the need of attacking myself in this connection, I cannot but regard all that pottering with stage properties as useless."

It has been customary in this country to speak of the play now presented to the public as "Countess Julie." The noble title is, of course, picturesque, but incorrect and unwarranted. It is, I fear, another outcome of that tendency to exploit the most sensational elements in Strindberg's art which has caused somebody to translate the name of his first great novel as "The Scarlet Room,"—instead of simply "The Red Room,"—thus hoping to connect it in the reader's mind with the scarlet woman of the Bible.

In Sweden, a countess is the wife or widow of a count. His daughter is no more a countess than is the daughter of an English earl. Her title is that of "Fröken," which corresponds exactly to the German "Fräulein" and the English "Miss." Once it was reserved for the young women of the nobility. By an agitation which shook all Sweden with mingled fury and mirth, it became extended to all unmarried women.

The French form of *Miss Julia's* Christian name is, on the other hand, in keeping with the author's intention, aiming at an expression of the foreign sympathies and manners which began to characterize the Swedish nobility in the eighteenth century, and which continued to assert themselves almost to the end of the nineteenth. But in English that form would not have the same significance, and nothing in the play makes its use imperative. The valet, on the other hand, would most appropriately be named *Jean* both in England and here, and for that reason I have retained this form of his name.

Almost every one translating from the Scandinavian languages insists on creating a difficulty out of the fact that the three northern nations—like the Germans and the French—still use the second person singular of the personal pronoun to indicate a closer degree of familiarity. But to translate the Swedish "du" with the English "thou" is as erroneous as it is awkward. Tytler laid down his "Principles of Translation" in 1791—and a majority of translators are still unaware of their existence. Yet it ought to seem self-evident to every thinking mind that idiomatic equivalence, not verbal identity, must form the basis of a good and faithful translation. When an English mother uses "you" to her child, she establishes thereby the only rational equivalent for the "du" used under similar circumstances by her Swedish sister.

Nobody familiar with the English language as it actually springs from the lips of living men and women can doubt that it offers ways of expressing varying shades of intimacy no less effective than any found in the Swedish tongue. Let me give an illustration from the play immediately under discussion. Returning to the stage after the ballet scene, *Jean* says to *Miss Julia:* "I love you—can you doubt it?" And her reply, literally, is: "You?—Say thou!" I have merely made him say: "Can you doubt it, Miss Julia?" and her answer: "Miss?—Call me Julia!" As that is just what would happen under similar circumstances among English-speaking people, I contend that not a whit of the author's meaning or spirit has been lost in this translation.

If ever a play was written for the stage, it is this one. And on the stage there is nothing to take the place of the notes and introductory explanations that so frequently encumber the printed volume. On the stage all explanations must lie within the play itself, and so they should in the book also, I believe. The translator is either an artist or a man unfit for his work. As an artist he must have a courage that cannot even be cowed by his reverence for the work of a great creative genius. If, mistakenly, he revere the letter of that work instead of its spirit, then he will reduce his own task to mere literary carpentry, and from his pen will spring not a living form, like the one he has been set to transplant, but only a death mask!

AUTHOR'S PREFACE

LIKE almost all other art, that of the stage has long seemed to me a sort of *Biblia Pauperum*, or a Bible in pictures for those who cannot read what is written or printed. And in the same way the playwright has seemed to me a lay preacher spreading the thoughts of his time in a form so popular that the middle classes, from which theatrical audiences are mainly drawn, can know what is being talked about without troubling their brains too much. For this reason the theatre has always served as a grammar-school to young people, women, and those who have acquired a little knowledge, all of whom retain the capacity for deceiving themselves and being deceived—which means again that they are susceptible to illusions produced by the suggestions of the author. And for the same reason I have had a feeling that, in our time, when the rudimentary, incomplete thought processes operating through our fancy seem to be developing into reflection, research, and analysis, the theatre might stand on the verge of being abandoned as a decaying form, for the enjoyment of which we lack the requisite conditions. The prolonged theatrical crisis now prevailing throughout Europe speaks in favour of such a supposition, as well as the fact that, in the civilised countries producing the greatest thinkers of the age, namely, England and Germany, the drama is as dead as are most of the other fine arts.

In some other countries it has, however, been thought possible to create a new drama by filling the old forms with the contents of a new time. But, for one thing, there has not been time for the new thoughts to become so popularized that the public might grasp the questions raised; secondly, minds have been so inflamed by party conflicts that pure and disinterested enjoyment has been excluded from places where one's innermost feelings are violated and the tyranny of an applauding or hissing majority is exercised with the openness for which the theatre gives a chance; and, finally, there has been no new form devised for the new contents, and the new wine has burst the old bottles.

In the following drama I have not tried to do anything new—for that cannot be done—but I have tried to modernize the form in accordance with the demands which I thought the new men of a new time might be likely to make on this art. And with such a purpose in view, I have chosen, or surrendered myself to, a theme that might well be said to lie outside the partisan strife of the day: for the problem of social ascendancy or decline, of higher or lower, of better or worse, of men or women, is, has been, and will be of lasting interest. In selecting this theme from real life, as it was related to me a number of years ago, when the incident impressed me very deeply, I found it suited to a tragedy, because it can only make us sad to see a fortunately placed individual perish, and this must be the case in still higher degree when we see an entire family die out. But perhaps a time will arrive when we have become so developed, so enlightened, that we can remain indifferent before the spectacle of life, which now seems so brutal, so cynical, so heartless; when we have closed up those lower, unreliable instruments of thought which we call feelings, and which have been rendered not only superfluous but harmful by the final growth of our reflective organs.

The fact that the heroine arouses our pity depends only on our weakness in not being able to resist the sense of fear that the same fate could befall ourselves. And yet it is possible that a very sensitive spectator might fail to find satisfaction in this kind of pity, while the man believing in the future might demand some positive suggestion for the abolition of evil, or, in other words, some kind of programme. But, first of all, there is no absolute evil. That one family perishes is the fortune of another family, which thereby gets a chance to rise. And the alternation of ascent and descent constitutes one of life's main charms, as fortune is solely determined by comparison. And to the man with a programme, who wants to remedy the sad circumstance that the hawk eats the dove, and the flea eats the hawk, I have this question to put: why should it be remedied? Life is not so mathematically idiotic that it lets only the big eat the small, but it happens just as often that the bee kills the lion, or drives it to madness at least.

That my tragedy makes a sad impression on many is their own fault. When we grow strong as were the men of the first French revolution, then we shall receive an unconditionally good and joyful impression from seeing the national forests rid of rotting and superannuated trees that have stood too long in the way of others with equal right to a period of free growth—an impression good in the same way as that received from the death of one incurably diseased.

Not long ago they reproached my tragedy "The Father" with being too sad—just as if they wanted merry tragedies. Everybody is clamouring arrogantly for "the joy of life," and all theatrical managers are giving orders for farces, as if the joy of life consisted in being silly and picturing all human beings as so many sufferers from St. Vitus' dance or idiocy. I find the joy of life in its violent and cruel struggles, and my pleasure lies in knowing something and learning something. And for this reason I have selected an unusual but instructive case— an exception, in a word—but a great exception, proving the rule, which, of course, will provoke all lovers of the commonplace. And what also will offend simple brains is that my action cannot be traced back to a single motive, that the view-point is not always the same. An event in real life—and this discovery is quite recent—springs generally from a whole series of more or less deep-lying motives, but of these the spectator chooses as a rule the one his reason can master most easily, or else the one reflecting most favourably on his power of reasoning. A suicide is committed. Bad business, says the merchant. Unrequited love, say the ladies. Sickness, says the sick man. Crushed hopes, says the shipwrecked. But now it may be that the motive lay in all or none of these directions. It is possible that the one who is dead may have hid the main motive by pushing forward another meant to place his memory in a better light.

In explanation of *Miss Julia's* sad fate I have suggested many factors: her mother's fundamental instincts; her father's mistaken upbringing of the girl; her own nature, and the suggestive influence of her fiancé on a weak and degenerate brain; furthermore, and more directly: the festive mood of the Midsummer Eve; the absence of her father; her physical condition; her preoccupation with the animals; the excitation of the dance; the dusk of the night; the strongly aphrodisiacal influence of the flowers; and lastly the chance forcing the two of them together in a secluded room, to which must be added the aggressiveness of the excited man.

Thus I have neither been one-sidedly physiological nor one-sidedly psychological in my procedure. Nor have I merely delivered a moral preachment. This multiplicity of motives I regard as praiseworthy because it is in keeping with the views of our own time. And if others have done the same thing before me, I may boast of not being the sole inventor of my paradoxes—as all discoveries are named.

In regard to the character-drawing I may say that I have tried to make my figures rather "characterless," and I have done so for reasons I shall now state.

In the course of the ages the word character has assumed many meanings. Originally it signified probably the dominant ground-note in the complex mass of the self, and as such it was confused with temperament. Afterward it became the middle-class term for an automaton, so that an individual whose nature had come to a stand still, or who had adapted himself to a certain part in life—who had ceased to grow, in a word—was named a character; while one remaining in a state of development—a skilful navigator on life's river, who did not sail with close-tied sheets, but knew when to fall off before the wind and when to luff again—was called lacking in character. And he was called so in a depreciatory sense, of course, because he was so hard to catch, to classify, and to keep track of. This middle-class notion about the immobility of the soul was transplanted to the stage, where the middle-class element has always held sway. There a character became synonymous with a gentleman fixed and finished once for all—one who invariably appeared drunk, jolly, sad. And for the purpose of characterisation nothing more was needed than some physical deformity like a clubfoot, a wooden leg, a red nose; or the person concerned was made to repeat some phrase like "That's capital!" or "Barkis is willin'," or something of that kind. This manner of regarding human beings as homogeneous is preserved even by the great Molière. *Harpagon* is nothing but miserly, although *Harpagon* might as well have been at once miserly and a financial genius, a fine father, and a public-spirited citizen. What is worse yet, his "defect" is of distinct advantage to his son-in-law and daughter, who are his heirs, and for that reason should not find fault with him, even if they have to wait a little for their wedding. I do not believe, therefore, in simple characters on the stage. And the summary judgments of the author upon men—this one stupid, and that one brutal, this one jealous, and that one stingy—should be challenged by the naturalists, who know the fertility of the soul-complex, and who realise that "vice" has a reverse very much resembling virtue.

Because they are modern characters, living in a period of transition more hysterically hurried than its immediate predecessor at least, I have made my figures vacillating, out of joint, torn between the old and the new. And I do not think it unlikely that, through newspaper reading and overheard conversations, modern ideas may have leaked down to the strata where domestic servants belong.

My souls (or characters) are conglomerates, made up of past and present stages of civilisation, scraps of humanity, torn-off pieces of Sunday clothing turned into rags—all patched together as is the human soul itself. And I have furthermore offered a touch of evolutionary history by letting the weaker repeat words stolen from the stronger, and by letting different souls accept "ideas"—or suggestions, as they are called—from each other.

Miss Julia is a modern character, not because the man-hating half-woman may not have existed in all ages, but because now, after her discovery, she has stepped to the front and begun to make a noise. The half-woman is a type coming more and more into prominence, selling herself nowadays for power, decorations, distinctions, diplomas, as formerly for money, and the type indicates degeneration. It is not a good type, for it does not last, but unfortunately it has the power of reproducing itself and its misery through one more generation. And degenerate men seem instinctively to make their selection from this kind of women, so that they multiply and produce indeterminate sexes to whom life is a torture. Fortunately, however, they perish in the end, either from discord with real life, or from the irresistible revolt of their suppressed instincts, or from foiled hopes of possessing the man. The type is tragical, offering us the spectacle of a desperate struggle against nature. It is also tragical as a Romantic inheritance dispersed by the prevailing Naturalism, which wants nothing but happiness: and for happiness strong and sound races are required.

But *Miss Julia* is also a remnant of the old military nobility which is now giving way to the new nobility of nerves and brain. She is a victim of the discord which a mother's "crime" produces in a family, and also a victim of the day's delusions, of the circumstances, of her defective constitution—all of which may be held equivalent to the old-fashioned fate or universal law. The naturalist has wiped out the idea of guilt, but he cannot wipe out the results of an action— punishment, prison, or fear—and for the simple reason that they remain without regard to his verdict. For fellow-beings that have been wronged are not so good-natured as those on the outside, who have not been wronged at all, can be without cost to themselves.

Even if, for reasons over which he could have no control, the father should forego his vengeance, the daughter would take vengeance upon herself, just as she does in the play, and she would be moved to it by that innate or acquired sense of honour which the upper classes inherit—whence? From the days of barbarism, from the original home of the Aryans, from the chivalry of the Middle Ages? It is beautiful, but it has become disadvantageous to the preservation of the race. It is this, the nobleman's *harakiri*—or the law of the inner conscience compelling the Japanese to cut open his own abdomen at the insult of another—which survives, though somewhat modified, in the duel, also a privilege of the nobility. For this reason the valet, *Jean*, continues to live, but *Miss Julia* cannot live on without honour. In so far as he lacks this life— endangering superstition about honour, the serf takes precedence of the earl, and in all of us Aryans there is something of the nobleman, or of Don Quixote, which makes us sympathise with the man who takes his own life because he has committed a dishonourable deed and thus lost his honour. And we are noblemen to the extent of suffering from seeing the earth littered with the living corpse of one who was once great—yes, even if the one thus fallen should rise again and make restitution by honourable deeds.

Jean, the valet, is of the kind that builds new stock—one in whom the differentiation is clearly noticeable. He was a cotter's child, and he has trained himself up to the point where the future gentleman has become visible. He has found it easy to learn, having finely developed senses (smell, taste, vision) and an instinct for beauty besides. He has already risen in the world, and is strong enough not to be sensitive about using other people's services. He has already become a stranger to his equals, despising them as so many outlived stages, but also fearing and fleeing them because they know his secrets, pry into his plans, watch his rise with envy, and look forward to his fall with pleasure. From this relationship springs his dual, indeterminate character, oscillating between love of distinction and hatred of those who have already achieved it. He says himself that he is an aristocrat, and has learned the secrets of good company. He is polished on the outside and coarse within. He knows already how to wear the frock-coat with ease, but the cleanliness of his body cannot be guaranteed.

He feels respect for the young lady, but he is afraid of *Christine*, who has his dangerous secrets in her keeping. His emotional callousness is sufficient to prevent the night's happenings from exercising a disturbing influence on his plans for the future. Having at once the slave's brutality and the master's lack of squeamishness, he can see blood without fainting, and he can also bend his back under a mishap until able to throw it off. For this reason he will emerge unharmed from the battle, and will probably end his days as the owner of a hotel. And if he does not become a Roumanian count, his son will probably go to a university, and may even become a county attorney.

Otherwise, he furnishes us with rather significant information as to the way in which the lower classes look at life from beneath— that is, when he speaks the truth, which is not often, as he prefers what seems favourable to himself to what is true. When *Miss Julia* suggests that the lower classes must feel the pressure from above very heavily, *Jean* agrees with her, of course, because he wants to gain her sympathy. But he corrects himself at once, the moment he realises the advantage of standing apart from the herd.

And *Jean* stands above *Miss Julia* not only because his fate is in ascendancy, but because he is a man. Sexually he is the aristocrat because of his male strength, his more finely developed senses, and his capacity for taking the initiative. His inferiority depends mainly on the temporary social environment in which he has to live, and which he probably can shed together with the valet's livery.

The mind of the slave speaks through his reverence for the count (as shown in the incident with the boots) and through his religious superstition. But he reveres the count principally as a possessor of that higher position toward which he himself is striving. And this reverence remains even when he has won the daughter of the house, and seen that the beautiful shell covered nothing but emptiness.

I don't believe that any love relation in a "higher" sense can spring up between two souls of such different quality. And for this reason I let *Miss Julia* imagine her love to be protective or commiserative in its origin. And I let *Jean* suppose that, under different social conditions, he might feel something like real love for her. I believe love to be like the hyacinth, which has to strike roots in darkness *before* it can bring forth a vigorous flower. In this case it shoots up quickly, bringing forth blossom and seed at once, and for that reason the plant withers so soon.

Christine, finally, is a female slave, full of servility and sluggishness acquired in front of the kitchen fire, and stuffed full of morality and religion that are meant to serve her at once as cloak and scapegoat. Her church-going has for its purpose to bring her quick and easy riddance of all responsibility for her domestic thieveries and to equip her with a new stock of guiltlessness. Otherwise she is a subordinate figure, and therefore purposely sketched in the same manner as the minister and the doctor in "The Father," whom I designed as ordinary human beings, like the common run of country ministers and country doctors. And if these accessory characters have seemed mere abstractions to some people, it depends on the fact that ordinary men are to a certain extent impersonal in the exercise of their callings. This means that they are without individuality, showing only one side of themselves while at work. And as long as the spectator does not feel the need of seeing them from other sides, my abstract presentation of them remains on the whole correct.

In regard to the dialogue, I want to point out that I have departed somewhat from prevailing traditions by not turning my figures into catechists who make stupid questions in order to call forth witty answers. I have avoided the symmetrical and mathematical construction of the French dialogue, and have instead permitted the minds to work irregularly as they do in reality, where, during conversation, the cogs of one mind seem more or less haphazardly to engage those of another one, and where no topic is fully exhausted. Naturally enough, therefore, the dialogue strays a good deal as, in the opening scenes, it acquires a material that later on is worked over, picked up again, repeated, expounded, and built up like the theme in a musical composition.

The plot is pregnant enough, and as, at bottom, it is concerned only with two persons, I have concentrated my attention on these, introducing only one subordinate figure, the cook, and keeping the unfortunate spirit of the father hovering above and beyond the action. I have done this because I believe I have noticed that the psychological processes are what interest the people of our own day more than anything else. Our souls, so eager for knowledge, cannot rest satisfied with seeing what happens, but must also learn how it comes to happen! What we want to see are just the wires, the machinery. We want to investigate the box with the false bottom, touch the magic ring in order to find the suture, and look into the cards to discover how they are marked.

In this I have taken for models the monographic novels of the brothers de Goncourt, which have appealed more to me than any other modern literature.

Turning to the technical side of the composition, I have tried to abolish the division into acts. And I have done so because I have come to fear that our decreasing capacity for illusion might be unfavourably affected by intermissions during which the spectator would have time to reflect and to get away from the suggestive influence of the author-hypnotist. My play will probably last an hour and a half, and as it is possible to listen that length of time, or longer, to a lecture, a sermon, or a debate, I have imagined that a theatrical performance could not become fatiguing in the same time. As early as 1872, in one of my first dramatic experiments, "The Outlaw," I tried the same concentrated form, but with scant success. The play was written in five acts and wholly completed when I became aware of the restless, scattered effect it produced. Then I burned it, and out of the ashes rose a single, well-built act, covering fifty printed pages, and taking hour for its performance. Thus the form of the present play is not new, but it seems to be my own, and changing aesthetical conventions may possibly make it timely.

My hope is still for a public educated to the point where it can sit through a whole-evening performance in a single act. But that point cannot be reached without a great deal of experimentation. In the meantime I have resorted to three art forms that are to provide resting-places for the public and the actors, without letting the public escape from the illusion induced. All these forms are subsidiary to the drama. They are the monologue, the pantomime, and the dance, all of them belonging originally to the tragedy of classical antiquity. For the monologue has sprung from the monody, and the chorus has developed into the ballet.

Our realists have excommunicated the monologue as improbable, but if I can lay a proper basis for it, I can also make it seem probable, and then I can use it to good advantage. It is probable, for instance, that a speaker may walk back and forth in his room practising his speech aloud; it is probable that an actor may read through his part aloud, that a servant-girl may talk to her cat, that a mother may prattle to her child, that an old spinster may chatter to her parrot, that a person may talk in his sleep. And in order that the actor for once may have a chance to work independently, and to be free for a moment from the author's pointer, it is better that the monologues be not written out, but just indicated. As it matters comparatively little what is said to the parrot or the cat, or in one's sleep—because it cannot influence the action—it is possible that a gifted actor, carried away by the situation and the mood of the occasion, may improvise such matters better than they could be written by the author, who cannot figure out in advance how much may be said, and how long the talk may last, without waking the public out of their illusions.

It is well known that, on certain stages, the Italian theatre has returned to improvisation and thereby produced creative actors— who, however, must follow the author's suggestions—and this may be counted a step forward, or even the beginning of a new art form that might well be called *productive*.

Where, on the other hand, the monologue would seem unreal, I have used the pantomime, and there I have left still greater scope for the actor's imagination—and for his desire to gain independent honours. But in order that the public may not be tried beyond endurance, I have permitted the music—which is amply warranted by the Midsummer Eve's dance—to exercise its illusory power while the dumb show lasts. And I ask the musical director to make careful selection of the music used for this purpose, so that incompatible moods are not induced by reminiscences from the last musical comedy or topical song, or by folk-tunes of too markedly ethnographical distinction.

The mere introduction of a scene with a lot of "people" could not have taken the place of the dance, for such scenes are poorly acted and tempt a number of grinning idiots into displaying their own smartness, whereby the illusion is disturbed. As the common people do not improvise their gibes, but use ready-made phrases in which stick some double meaning, I have not composed their lampooning song, but have appropriated a little known folk-dance which I personally noted down in a district near Stockholm. The words don't quite hit the point, but hint vaguely at it, and this is intentional, for the cunning (i. e., weakness) of the slave keeps him from any direct attack. There must, then, be no chattering clowns in a serious action, and no coarse flouting at a situation that puts the lid on the coffin of a whole family.

As far as the scenery is concerned, I have borrowed from impressionistic painting its asymmetry, its quality of abruptness, and have thereby in my opinion strengthened the illusion. Because the whole room and all its contents are not shown, there is a chance to guess at things—that is, our imagination is stirred into complementing our vision. I have made a further gain in getting rid of those tiresome exits by means of doors, especially as stage doors are made of canvas and swing back and forth at the lightest touch. They are not even capable of expressing the anger of an irate *pater familias* who, on leaving his home after a poor dinner, slams the door behind him "so that it shakes the whole house." (On the stage the house sways.) I have also contented myself with a single setting, and for the double purpose of making the figures become parts of their surroundings, and of breaking with the tendency toward luxurious scenery. But having only a single setting, one may demand to have it real. Yet nothing is more difficult than to get a room that looks something like a room, although the painter can easily enough produce waterfalls and flaming volcanoes. Let it go at canvas for the walls, but we might be done with the painting of shelves and kitchen utensils on the canvas. We have so much else on the stage that is conventional, and in which we are asked to believe, that we might at least be spared the too great effort of believing in painted pans and kettles.

I have placed the rear wall and the table diagonally across the stage in order to make the actors show full face and half profile to the audience when they sit opposite each other at the table. In the opera "Aïda" I noticed an oblique background, which led the eye out into unseen prospects. And it did not appear to be the result of any reaction against the fatiguing right angle.

Another novelty well needed would be the abolition of the foot-lights. The light from below is said to have for its purpose to make the faces of the actors look fatter. But I cannot help asking: why must all actors be fat in the face? Does not this light from below tend to wipe out the subtler lineaments in the lower part of the face, and especially around the jaws? Does it not give a false appearance to the nose and cast shadows upward over the eyes? If this be not so, another thing is certain: namely, that the eyes of the actors suffer from the light, so that the effective play of their glances is precluded. Coming from below, the light strikes the retina in places generally protected (except in sailors, who have to see the sun reflected in the water), and for this reason one observes hardly anything but a vulgar rolling of the eyes, either sideways or upwards, toward the galleries, so that nothing but the white of the eye shows. Perhaps the same cause may account for the tedious blinking of which especially the actresses are guilty. And when anybody on the stage wants to use his eyes to speak with, no other way is left him but the poor one of staring straight at the public, with whom he or she then gets into direct communication outside of the frame provided by the setting. This vicious habit has, rightly or wrongly, been named "to meet friends." Would it not be possible by means of strong side-lights (obtained by the employment of reflectors, for instance) to add to the resources already possessed by the actor? Could not his mimicry be still further strengthened by use of the greatest asset possessed by the face: the play of the eyes?

Of course, I have no illusions about getting the actors to play *for* the public and not *at* it, although such a change would be highly desirable. I dare not even dream of beholding the actor's back throughout an important scene, but I wish with all my heart that crucial scenes might not be played in the centre of the proscenium, like duets meant to bring forth applause. Instead, I should like to have them laid in the place indicated by the situation. Thus I ask for no revolutions, but only for a few minor modifications. To make a real room of the stage, with the fourth wall missing, and a part of the furniture placed back toward the audience, would probably produce a disturbing effect at present.

In wishing to speak of the facial make-up, I have no hope that the ladies will listen to me, as they would rather look beautiful than lifelike. But the actor might consider whether it be to his advantage to paint his face so that it shows some abstract type which covers it like a mask. Suppose that a man puts a markedly choleric line between the eyes, and imagine further that some remark demands a smile of this face fixed in a state of continuous wrath. What a horrible grimace will be the result? And how can the wrathful old man produce a frown on his false forehead, which is smooth as a billiard ball?

In modern psychological dramas, where the subtlest movements of the soul are to be reflected on the face rather than by gestures and noise, it would probably be well to experiment with strong side-light on a small stage, and with unpainted faces, or at least with a minimum of make-up.

If, in additon, we might escape the visible orchestra, with its disturbing lamps and its faces turned toward the public; if we could have the seats on the main floor (the orchestra or the pit) raised so that the eyes of the spectators would be above the knees of the actors; if we could get rid of the boxes with their tittering parties of diners; if we could also have the auditorium completely darkened during the performance; and if, first and last, we could have a small stage and a small house: then a new dramatic art might rise, and the theatre might at least become an institution for the entertainment of people with culture. While waiting for this kind of theatre, I suppose we shall have to write for the "ice-box," and thus prepare the repertory that is to come.

I have made an attempt. If it prove a failure, there is plenty of time to try over again.

MISS JULIA
A NATURALISTIC TRAGEDY
1888

PERSONS

MISS JULIA, aged twenty-five
JEAN, a valet, aged thirty
CHRISTINE, a cook, aged thirty-five

    The action takes place on Midsummer Eve, in the kitchen of the count's country house.

MISS JULIA

SCENE

(A large kitchen: the ceiling and the side walls are hidden by draperies and hangings. The rear wall runs diagonally across the stage, from the left side and away from the spectators. On this wall, to the left, there are two shelves full of utensils made of copper, iron, and tin. The shelves are trimmed with scalloped paper.)

(A little to the right may be seen three fourths of the big arched doorway leading to the outside. It has double glass doors, through which are seen a fountain with a cupid, lilac shrubs in bloom, and the tops of some Lombardy poplars.)

(On the left side of the stage is seen the corner of a big cook stove built of glazed bricks; also a part of the smoke-hood above it.)

(From the right protrudes one end of the servants' dining-table of white pine, with a few chairs about it.)

(The stove is dressed with bundled branches of birch. Twigs of juniper are scattered on the floor.)

(On the table end stands a big Japanese spice pot full of lilac blossoms.)

(An icebox, a kitchen-table, and a wash-stand.)

(Above the door hangs a big old-fashioned bell on a steel spring, and the mouthpiece of a speaking-tube appears at the left of the door.)

(CHRISTINE is standing by the stove, frying something in a pan. She has on a dress of light-coloured cotton, which she has covered up with a big kitchen apron.)

(JEAN enters, dressed in livery and carrying a pair of big, spurred riding boots, which he places on the floor in such manner that they remain visible to the spectators.)

JEAN. To-night Miss Julia is crazy again; absolutely crazy.

CHRISTINE. So you're back again?

JEAN. I took the count to the station, and when I came back by the barn, I went in and had a dance, and there I saw the young lady leading the dance with the gamekeeper. But when she caught sight of me, she rushed right up to me and asked me to dance the ladies' waltz with her. And ever since she's been waltzing like—well, I never saw the like of it. She's crazy!

CHRISTINE. And has always been, but never the way it's been this last fortnight, since her engagement was broken.

JEAN. Well, what kind of a story was that anyhow? He's a fine fellow, isn't he, although he isn't rich? Ugh, but they're so full of notions. [Sits down at the end of the table] It's peculiar anyhow, that a young lady—hm!—would rather stay at home with the servants—don't you think?—than go with her father to their relatives!

CHRISTINE. Oh, I guess she feels sort of embarrassed by that rumpus with her fellow.

JEAN. Quite likely. But there was some backbone to that man just the same. Do you know how it happened, Christine? I saw it, although I didn't care to let on.

CHRISTINE. No, did you?

JEAN. Sure, I did. They were in the stable-yard one evening, and the young lady was training him, as she called it. Do you know what that meant? She made him leap over her horse-whip the way you teach a dog to jump. Twice he jumped and got a cut each time. The third time he took the whip out of her hand and broke it into a thousand bits. And then he got out.

CHRISTINE. So that's the way it happened! You don't say!

JEAN. Yes, that's how that thing happened. Well, Christine, what have you got that's tasty?

CHRISTINE. [Serves from the pan and puts the plate before Jean] Oh, just some kidney which I cut out of the veal roast.

JEAN. [Smelling the food] Fine! That's my great *délice*. [Feeling the plate] But you might have warmed the plate.

CHRISTINE. Well, if you ain't harder to please than the count himself! [Pulls his hair playfully.]

JEAN. [Irritated] Don't pull my hair! You know how sensitive I am.

CHRISTINE. Well, well, it was nothing but a love pull, you know.

[JEAN eats.]

[CHRISTINE opens a bottle of beer.]

JEAN. Beer-on Midsummer Eve? No, thank you! Then I have something better myself. [Opens a table-drawer and takes out a bottle of claret with yellow cap] Yellow seal, mind you! Give me a glass——and you use those with stems when you drink it *pure*.

CHRISTINE. [Returns to the stove and puts a small pan on the fire] Heaven preserve her that gets you for a husband, Mr. Finicky!

JEAN. Oh, rot! You'd be glad enough to get a smart fellow like me. And I guess it hasn't hurt you that they call me your beau. [Tasting the wine] Good! Pretty good! Just a tiny bit too cold. [He warms the glass with his hand.] We got this at Dijon. It cost us four francs per litre, not counting the bottle. And there was the duty besides. What is it you're cooking—with that infernal smell?

CHRISTINE. Oh, it's some deviltry the young lady is going to give Diana.

JEAN. You should choose your words with more care, Christine. But why should you be cooking for a bitch on a holiday eve like this? Is she sick?

CHRISTINE. Ye-es, she is sick. She's been running around with the gate-keeper's pug—and now's there's trouble—and the young lady just won't hear of it.

JEAN. The young lady is too stuck up in some ways and not proud enough in others—just as was the countess while she lived. She was most at home in the kitchen and among the cows, but she would never drive with only one horse. She wore her cuffs till they were dirty, but she had to have cuff buttons with a coronet on them. And speaking of the young lady, she doesn't take proper care of herself and her person. I might even say that she's lacking in refinement. Just now, when she was dancing in the barn, she pulled the gamekeeper away from

Anna and asked him herself to come and dance with her. We wouldn't act in that way. But that's just how it is: when upper-class people want to demean themselves, then they grow—— mean! But she's splendid! Magnificent! Oh, such shoulders! And—and so on!

CHRISTINE. Oh, well, don't brag too much! I've heard Clara talking, who tends to her dressing.

JEAN. Pooh, Clara! You're always jealous of each other. I, who have been out riding with her—And then the way she dances!

CHRISTINE. Say, Jean, won't you dance with me when I'm done?

JEAN. Of course I will.

CHRISTINE. Do you promise?

JEAN. Promise? When I say so, I'll do it. Well, here's thanks for the good food. It tasted fine! [Puts the cork back into the bottle.]

JULIA. [Appears in the doorway, speaking to somebody on the outside] I'll be back in a minute. You go right on in the meantime.

[JEAN slips the bottle into the table-drawer and rises respectfully.]

JULIA.[Enters and goes over to CHRISTINE by the wash-stand] Well, is it done yet?

[CHRISTINE signs to her that JEAN is present.]

JEAN. [Gallantly] The ladies are having secrets, I believe.

JULIA. [Strikes him in the face with her handkerchief] That's for you, Mr. Pry!

JEAN. Oh, what a delicious odor that violet has!

JULIA. [With coquetry] Impudent! So you know something about perfumes also? And know pretty well how to dance—Now don't peep! Go away!

JEAN. [With polite impudence] Is it some kind of witches' broth the ladies are cooking on Midsummer Eve—something to tell fortunes by and bring out the lucky star in which one's future love is seen?

JULIA. [Sharply] If you can see that, you'll have good eyes, indeed! [To CHRISTINE] Put it in a pint bottle and cork it well. Come and dance a *schottische* with me now, Jean.

JEAN. [Hesitatingly] I don't want to be impolite, but I had promised to dance with Christine this time——

JULIA. Well, she can get somebody else—can't you, Christine? Won't you let me borrow Jean from you?

CHRISTINE. That isn't for me to say. When Miss Julia is so gracious, it isn't for him to say no. You just go along, and be thankful for the honour, too!

JEAN. Frankly speaking, but not wishing to offend in any way, I cannot help wondering if it's wise for Miss Julia to dance twice in succession with the same partner, especially as the people here are not slow in throwing out hints—

JULIA. [Flaring up] What is that? What kind of hints? What do you mean?

JEAN. [Submissively] As you don't want to understand, I have to speak more plainly. It don't look well to prefer one servant to all the rest who are expecting to be honoured in the same unusual way—

JULIA. Prefer! What ideas! I'm surprised! I, the mistress of the house, deign to honour this dance with my presence, and when it so happens that I actually want to dance, I want to dance with one who knows how to lead, so that I am not made ridiculous.

JEAN. As you command, Miss Julia! I am at your service!

JULIA. [Softened] Don't take it as a command. To-night we should enjoy ourselves as a lot of happy people, and all rank should be forgotten. Now give me your arm. Don't be afraid, Christine! I'll return your beau to you!

[JEAN offers his arm to MISS JULIA and leads her out.]

* * *

PANTOMIME

Must be acted as if the actress were really alone in the place. When necessary she turns her back to the public. She should not look in the direction of the spectators, and she should not hurry as if fearful that they might become impatient.

CHRISTINE is alone. A *schottische* tune played on a violin is heard faintly in the distance.

While humming the tune, CHRISTINE clears o$ the table after JEAN, washes the plate at the kitchen table, wipes it, and puts it away in a cupboard.

Then she takes of her apron, pulls out a small mirror from one of the table-drawers and leans it against the flower jar on the table; lights a tallow candle and heats a hairpin, which she uses to curl her front hair.

Then she goes to the door and stands there listening. Returns to the table. Discovers the handkerchief which MISS JULIA has left behind, picks it up, and smells it, spreads it out absent-mindedly and begins to stretch it, smooth it, fold it up, and so forth.

* * *

JEAN. [Enters alone] Crazy, that's what she is! The way she dances! And the people stand behind the doors and grill at her. What do you think of it, Christine?

CHRISTINE. Oh, she has her time now, and then she is always a little queer like that. But are you going to dance with me now?

JEAN. You are not mad at me because I disappointed you?

CHRISTINE. No!—Not for a little thing like that, you know! And also, I know my place—

JEAN. [Putting his arm around her waist] You are a, sensible girl, Christine, and I think you'll make a good wife—

JULIA. [Enters and is unpleasantly surprised; speaks with forced gayety] Yes, you are a fine partner—running away from your lady!

JEAN. On the contrary, Miss Julia. I have, as you see, looked up the one I deserted.

JULIA. [Changing tone] Do you know, there is nobody that dances like you!—But why do you wear your livery on an evening like this? Take it off at once!

JEAN. Then I must ask you to step outside for a moment, as my black coat is hanging right here. [Points toward the right and goes in that direction.]

JULIA. Are you bashful on my account? Just to change a coat? Why don't you go into your own room and come back again? Or, you can stay right here, and I'll turn my back on you.

JEAN. With your permission, Miss Julia. [Goes further over to the right; one of his arms can be seen as he changes his coat.]

JULIA [To CHRISTINE] Are you and Jean engaged, that he's so familiar with you?

CHRISTINE. Engaged? Well, in a way. We call it that.

JULIA. Call it?

CHRISTINE. Well, Miss Julia, you have had a fellow of your own, and—

JULIA. We were really engaged—

CHRISTINE. But it didn't come to anything just the same—

[JEAN enters, dressed in black frock coat and black derby.]

JULIA. *Très gentil, Monsieur Jean! Très gentil!*

JEAN. *Vous voulez plaisanter, Madame!*

JULIA. *Et vous voulez parler français!* Where did you learn it?

JEAN. In Switzerland, while I worked as *sommelier* in one of the big hotels at Lucerne.

JULIA. But you look like a real gentleman in your frock coat! Charming! [Sits down at the table.]

JEAN. Oh, you flatter me.

JULIA. [Offended] Flatter—you!

JEAN. My natural modesty does not allow me to believe that you could be paying genuine compliments to one like me, and so I dare to assume that you are exaggerating, or, as we call it, flattering.

JULIA. Where did you learn to use your words like that? You must have been to the theatre a great deal?

JEAN. That, too. I have been to a lot of places.

JULIA. But you were born in this neighbourhood?

JEAN. My father was a cotter on the county attorney's property right by here, and I can recall seeing you as a child, although you, of course, didn't notice me.

JULIA. No, really!

JEAN. Yes, and I remember one time in particular—but of that I can't speak.

JULIA. Oh, yes, do! Why—just for once.

JEAN. No, really, I cannot do it now. Another time, perhaps.

JULIA. Another time is no time. Is it as bad as that?

JEAN. It isn't bad, but it comes a little hard. Look at that one! [Points to CHRISTINE, who has fallen asleep on a chair by the stove.]

JULIA. She'll make a pleasant wife. And perhaps she snores, too.

JEAN. No, she doesn't, but she talks in her sleep.

JULIA. [Cynically] How do you know?

JEAN. [Insolently] I have heard it.

[Pause during which they study each other.]

JULIA. Why don't you sit down?

JEAN. It wouldn't be proper in your presence.

JULIA. But if I order you to do it?

JEAN. Then I obey.

JULIA. Sit down, then!—But wait a moment! Can you give me something to drink first?

JEAN. I don't know what we have got in the icebox. I fear it is nothing but beer.

JULIA. And you call that nothing? My taste is so simple that I prefer it to wine.

JEAN. [Takes a bottle of beer from the icebox and opens it; gets a glass and a plate from the cupboard, and serves the beer] Allow me!

JULIA. Thank you. Don't you want some yourself?

JEAN. I don't care very much for beer, but if it is a command, of course—

JULIA. Command?—I should think a polite gentleman might keep his lady company.

JEAN. Yes, that's the way it should be. [Opens another bottle and takes out a glass.]

JULIA. Drink my health now!

[JEAN hesitates.]

JULIA. Are you bashful—a big, grown-up man?

JEAN. [Kneels with mock solemnity and raises his glass] To the health of my liege lady!

JULIA. Bravo!—And now you must also kiss my shoe in order to get it just right.

[JEAN hesitates a moment; then he takes hold of her foot and touches it lightly with his lips.]

JULIA. Excellent! You should have been on the stage.

JEAN. [Rising to his feet] This won't do any longer, Miss Julia. Somebody might see us.

JULIA. What would that matter?

JEAN. Oh, it would set the people talking—that's all! And if you only knew how their tongues were wagging up there a while ago——

JULIA. What did they have to say? Tell me—Sit down now!

JEAN. [Sits down] I don't want to hurt you, but they were using expressions—which cast reflections of a kind that—oh, you know it yourself! You are not a child, and when a lady is seen alone with a man, drinking—no matter if he's only a servant—and at night——then—

JULIA. Then what? And besides, we are not alone. Isn't Christine with us?

JEAN. Yes—asleep!

JULIA. Then I'll wake her. [Rising] Christine, are you asleep?

CHRISTINE. [In her sleep] Blub-blub-blub-blub!

JULIA. Christine!—Did you ever see such a sleeper.

CHRISTINE. [In her sleep] The count's boots are polished—put on the coffee—yes, yes, yes—my-my—pooh!

JULIA. [Pinches her nose] Can't you wake up?

JEAN. [Sternly] You shouldn't bother those that sleep.

JULIA. [Sharply] What's that?

JEAN. One who has stood by the stove all day has a right to be tired at night. And sleep should be respected.

JULIA. [Changing tone] It is fine to think like that, and it does you honour—I thank you for it. [Gives JEAN her hand] Come now and pick some lilacs for me.

[During the following scene CHRISTINE wakes up. She moves as if still asleep and goes out to the right in order to go to bed.]

JEAN. With you, Miss Julia?

JULIA. With me!

JEAN. But it won't do! Absolutely not!

JULIA. I can't understand what you are thinking of. You couldn't possibly imagine—

JEAN. No, not I, but the people.

JULIA. What? That I am fond of the valet?

JEAN. I am not at all conceited, but such things have happened—and to the people nothing is sacred.

JULIA. You are an aristocrat, I think.

JEAN. Yes, I am.

JULIA. And I am stepping down—

JEAN. Take my advice, Miss Julia, don't step down. Nobody will believe you did it on purpose. The people will always say that you fell down.

JULIA. I think better of the people than you do. Come and see if I am not right. Come along! [She ogles him.]

JEAN. You're mighty queer, do you know!

JULIA. Perhaps. But so are you. And for that matter, everything is queer. Life, men, everything—just a mush that floats on top of the water until it sinks, sinks down! I have a dream that comes back to me ever so often. And just now I am reminded of it. I have climbed to the top of a column and sit there without being able to tell how to get down again. I get dizzy when I look down, and I must get down, but I haven't the courage to jump off. I cannot hold on, and I am longing to fall, and yet I don't fall. But there will be no rest for me until I get down, no rest until I get down, down on the ground. And if I did reach the ground, I should want to get still further down, into the ground itself—Have you ever felt like that?

JEAN. No, my dream is that I am lying under a tall tree in a dark wood. I want to get up, up to the top, so that I can look out over the smiling landscape, where the sun is shining, and so that I can rob the nest in which lie the golden eggs. And I climb and climb, but the trunk is so thick and smooth, and it is so far to the first branch. But I know that if I could only reach that first branch, then I should go right on to the top as on a ladder. I have not reached it yet, but I am going to, if it only be in my dreams.

JULIA. Here I am chattering to you about dreams! Come along! Only into the park! [She offers her arm to him, and they go toward the door.]

JEAN. We must sleep on nine midsummer flowers to-night, Miss Julia——then our dreams will come true.

[They turn around in the doorway, and JEAN puts one hand up to his eyes.]

JULIA. Let me see what you have got in your eye.

JEAN. Oh, nothing—just some dirt—it will soon be gone.

JULIA. It was my sleeve that rubbed against it. Sit down and let me help you. [Takes him by the arm and makes him sit down; takes hold of his head and bends it backwards; tries to get out the dirt with a corner of her handkerchief] Sit still now, absolutely still! [Slaps him on the hand] Well, can't you do as I say? I think you are shaking—a big, strong fellow like you! [Feels his biceps] And with such arms!

JEAN. [Ominously] Miss Julia!

JULIA. Yes, Monsieur Jean.

JEAN. *Attention! Je ne suis qu'un homme.*

JULIA. Can't you sit still!—There now! Now it's gone. Kiss my hand now, and thank me.

JEAN. [Rising] Miss Julia, listen to me. Christine has gone to bed now—Won't you listen to me?

JULIA. Kiss my hand first.

JEAN. Listen to me!

JULIA. Kiss my hand first!

JEAN. All right, but blame nobody but yourself!

JULIA. For what?

JEAN. For what? Are you still a mere child at twenty-five? Don't you know that it is dangerous to play with fire?

JULIA. Not for me. I am insured.

JEAN. [Boldly] No, you are not. And even if you were, there are inflammable surroundings to be counted with.

JULIA. That's you, I suppose?

JEAN. Yes. Not because I am I, but because I am a young man—

JULIA. Of handsome appearance—what an incredible conceit! A Don Juan, perhaps. Or a Joseph? On my soul, I think you are a Joseph!

JEAN. Do you?

JULIA. I fear it almost.

[JEAN goes boldly up to her and takes her around the waist in order to kiss her.]

JULIA. [Gives him a cuff on the ear] Shame!

JEAN. Was that in play or in earnest?

JULIA. In earnest.

JEAN. Then you were in earnest a moment ago also. Your playing is too serious, and that's the dangerous thing about it. Now I am tired of playing, and I ask to be excused in order to resume my work. The count wants his boots to be ready for him, and it is after midnight already.

JULIA. Put away the boots.

JEAN. No, it's my work, which I am bound to do. But I have not undertaken to be your playmate. It's something I can never become—- I hold myself too good for it.

JULIA. You're proud!

JEAN. In some ways, and not in others.

JULIA. Have you ever been in love?

JEAN. We don't use that word. But I have been fond of a lot of girls, and once I was taken sick because I couldn't have the one I wanted: sick, you know, like those princes in the Arabian Nights who cannot eat or drink for sheer love.

JULIA. Who was it?

[JEAN remains silent.]

JULIA. Who was it?

JEAN. You cannot make me tell you.

JULIA. If I ask you as an equal, ask you as—a friend: who was it?

JEAN. It was you.

JULIA. [Sits down] How funny!

JEAN. Yes, as you say—it was ludicrous. That was the story, you see, which I didn't want to tell you a while ago. But now I am going to tell it. Do you know how the world looks from below—no, you don't. No more than do hawks and falcons, of whom we never see the back because they are always floating about high up in the sky. I lived in the cotter's hovel, together with seven other children, and a pig—out there on the grey plain, where there isn't a single tree. But from our windows I could see the wall around the count's park, and apple-trees above it. That was the Garden of Eden, and many fierce angels were guarding it with flaming swords. Nevertheless I and some other boys found our way to the Tree of Life—now you despise me?

JULIA. Oh, stealing apples is something all boys do.

JEAN. You may say so now, but you despise me nevertheless. However—- once I got into the Garden of Eden with my mother to weed the onion beds. Near by stood a Turkish pavillion, shaded by trees and covered with honeysuckle. I didn't know what it was used for, but I had never seen a more beautiful building. People went in and came out again, and one day the door was left wide open. I stole up and saw the walls covered with pictures of kings and emperors, and the windows were hung with red, fringed curtains—now you know what I mean. I—[breaks off a lilac sprig and holds it under MISS JULIA's nose]—I had never been inside the manor, and I had never seen anything but the church—and this was much finer. No matter where my thoughts ran, they returned always—to that place. And gradually a longing arose within me to taste the full pleasure of—*enfin*! I sneaked in, looked and admired. Then I heard somebody coming. There was only one way out for fine people, but for me there was another, and I could do nothing else but choose it.

[JULIA, who has taken the lilac sprig, lets it drop on the table.]

JEAN. Then I started to run, plunged through a hedge of raspberry bushes, chased right across a strawberry plantation, and came out on the terrace where the roses grow. There I caught sight of a pink dress and pair of white stockings—that was you! I crawled under a pile of weeds—right into it, you know—into stinging thistles and wet, ill-smelling dirt. And I saw you walking among the roses, and I thought: if it be possible for a robber to get into heaven and dwell with the angels, then it is strange that a cotter's child, here on God's own earth, cannot get into the park and play with the count's daughter.

JULIA. [Sentimentally] Do you think all poor children have the same thoughts as you had in this case?

JEAN. [Hesitatingly at first; then with conviction] If *all* poor— yes—-of course. Of course!

JULIA. It must be a dreadful misfortune to be poor.

JEAN. [In a tone of deep distress and with rather exaggerated emphasis] Oh, Miss Julia! Oh!—A dog may lie on her ladyship's sofa; a horse may have his nose patted by the young lady's hand, but a servant—[changing his tone]—oh well, here and there you meet one made of different stuff, and he makes a way for himself in the world, but how often does it happen?—However, do you know what I did? I jumped into the mill brook with my clothes on, and was pulled out, and got a licking. But the next Sunday, when my father and the rest of the people were going over to my grandmother's, I fixed it so that I could stay at home. And then I washed myself with soap and hot water, and put on my best clothes, and went to church, where I could see you. I did see you, and went home determined to die. But I wanted to die beautifully and pleasantly, without any pain. And then I recalled that it was dangerous to sleep under an elder bush. We had a big one that was in full bloom. I robbed it of all its flowers, and then I put them in the big box where the oats were kept and lay down in them. Did you ever notice the smoothness of oats? Soft to the touch as the skin of the human body! However, I pulled down the lid and closed my eyes—fell asleep and was waked up a very sick boy. But I didn't die, as you can see. What I wanted—that's more than I can tell. Of course, there was not the least hope of winning you——but you symbolised the hopelessness of trying to get out of the class into which I was born.

JULIA. You narrate splendidly, do you know! Did you ever go to school?

JEAN. A little. But I have read a lot of novels and gone to the theatre a good deal. And besides, I have listened to the talk of better-class people, and from that I have learned most of all.

JULIA. Do you stand around and listen to what we are saying?

JEAN. Of course! And I have heard a lot, too, when I was on the box of the carriage, or rowing the boat. Once I heard you, Miss Julia, and one of your girl friends—

JULIA. Oh!—What was it you heard then?

JEAN. Well, it wouldn't be easy to repeat. But I was rather surprised, and I couldn't understand where you had learned all those words. Perhaps, at bottom, there isn't quite so much difference as they think between one kind of people and another.

JULIA. You ought to be ashamed of yourself! We don't live as you do when we are engaged.

JEAN. [Looking hard at her] Is it so certain?—Well, Miss Julia, it won't pay to make yourself out so very innocent to me——

JULIA. The man on whom I bestowed my love was a scoundrel.

JEAN. That's what you always say—afterwards.

JULIA. Always?

JEAN. Always, I believe, for I have heard the same words used several times before, on similar occasions.

JULIA. What occasions?

JEAN. Like the one of which we were speaking. The last time—

JULIA. [Rising] Stop! I don't want to hear any more!

JEAN. Nor did *she*—curiously enough! Well, then I ask permission to go to bed.

JULIA. [Gently] Go to bed on Midsummer Eve?

JEAN. Yes, for dancing with that mob out there has really no attraction for me.

JULIA. Get the key to the boat and take me out on the lake—I want to watch the sunrise.

JEAN. Would that be wise?

JULIA. It sounds as if you were afraid of your reputation.

JEAN. Why not? I don't care to be made ridiculous, and I don't care to be discharged without a recommendation, for I am trying to get on in the world. And then I feel myself under a certain obligation to Christine.

JULIA. So it's Christine now

JEAN. Yes, but it's you also—Take my advice and go to bed!

JULIA. Am I to obey you?

JEAN. For once—and for your own sake! The night is far gone. Sleepiness makes us drunk, and the head grows hot. Go to bed! And besides—if I am not mistaken——I can hear the crowd coming this way to look for me. And if we are found together here, you are lost!

> CHORUS. [Is heard approaching]:
> Through the fields come two ladies a-walking,
> Treederee-derallah, treederee-derah.
> And one has her shoes full of water,
> Treederee-derallah-lah.
>
> They're talking of hundreds of dollars,
> Treederee-derallah, treederee-derah.
> But have not between them a dollar
> Treederee-derallah-lah.
>
> This wreath I give you gladly,
> Treederee-derallah, treederee-derah.
> But love another madly,
> Treederee-derallah-lah.

JULIA. I know the people, and I love them, just as they love me. Let them come, and you'll see.

JEAN. No, Miss Julia, they don't love you. They take your food and spit at

your back. Believe me. Listen to me—can't you hear what they are singing?—
No, don't pay any attention to it!

JULIA. [Listening] What is it they are singing?

JEAN. Oh, something scurrilous. About you and me.

JULIA. How infamous! They ought to be ashamed! And the treachery of it!

JEAN. The mob is always cowardly. And in such a fight as this there is
nothing to do but to run away.

JULIA. Run away? Where to? We cannot get out. And we cannot go into
Christine's room.

JEAN. Oh, we cannot? Well, into my room, then! Necessity knows no law.
And you can trust me, for I am your true and frank and respectful friend.

JULIA. But think only-think if they should look for you in there!

JEAN. I shall bolt the door. And if they try to break it I open, I'll shoot!—
Come! [Kneeling before her] Come!

JULIA. [Meaningly] And you promise me—?

JEAN. I swear!

[MISS JULIA goes quickly out to the right. JEAN follows her eagerly.]

                                  * * *

BALLET

The peasants enter. They are decked out in their best and carry flowers in
their hats. A fiddler leads them. On the table they place a barrel of small-beer
and a keg of "brännvin," or white Swedish whiskey, both of them decorated
with wreathes woven out of leaves. First they drink. Then they form in ring and
sing and dance to the melody heard before:

    "Through the fields come two ladies a-walking."

The dance finished, they leave singing.

                                  * * *

JULIA. [Enters alone. On seeing the disorder in the kitchen, she claps her
hands together. Then she takes out a powder-puff and begins to powder her face.]

JEAN. [Enters in a state of exaltation] There you see! And you heard, didn't
you? Do you think it possible to stay here?

JULIA. No, I don't think so. But what are we to do?

JEAN. Run away, travel, far away from here.

JULIA. Travel? Yes-but where?

JEAN. To Switzerland, the Italian lakes—you have never been there?

JULIA. No. Is the country beautiful?

JEAN. Oh! Eternal summer! Orange trees! Laurels! Oh!

JULIA. But then-what are we to do down there?

JEAN. I'll start a hotel, everything first class, including the customers?

JULIA. Hotel?

JEAN. That's the life, I tell you! Constantly new faces and new languages.
Never a minute free for nerves or brooding. No trouble about what to do—for
the work is calling to be done: night and day, bells that ring, trains that whistle,
'busses that come and go; and gold pieces raining on the counter all the time.
That's the life for you!

JULIA. Yes, that is life. And I?

JEAN. The mistress of everything, the chief ornament of the house. With your looks—and your manners—oh, success will be assured! Enormous! You'll sit like a queen in the office and keep the slaves going by the touch of an electric button. The guests will pass in review before your throne and timidly deposit their treasures on your table. You cannot imagine how people tremble when a bill is presented to them—I'll salt the items, and you'll sugar them with your sweetest smiles. Oh, let us get away from here—[pulling a time-table from his pocket]—at once, with the next train! We'll be in Malmö at 6.30; in Hamburg at 8.40 to-morrow morning; in Frankfort and Basel a day later. And to reach Como by way of the St. Gotthard it will take us—let me see—three days. Three days!

JULIA. All that is all right. But you must give me some courage— Jean. Tell me that you love me. Come and take me in your arms.

JEAN. [Reluctantly] I should like to—but I don't dare. Not in this house again. I love you—beyond doubt—or, can you doubt it, Miss Julia?

JULIA. [With modesty and true womanly feeling] Miss? Call me Julia. Between us there can be no barriers here after. Call me Julia!

JEAN. [Disturbed] I cannot! There will be barriers between us as long as we stay in this house—there is the past, and there is the count——and I have never met another person for whom I felt such respect. If I only catch sight of his gloves on a chair I feel small. If I only hear that bell up there, I jump like a shy horse. And even now, when I see his boots standing there so stiff and perky, it is as if something made my back bend. [Kicking at the boots] It's nothing but superstition and tradition hammered into us from childhood—but it can be as easily forgotten again. Let us only get to another country, where they have a republic, and you'll see them bend their backs double before my liveried porter. You see, backs have to be bent, but not mine. I wasn't born to that kind of thing. There's better stuff in me—character—and if I only get hold of the first branch, you'll see me do some climbing. To-day I am a valet, but next year I'll be a hotel owner. In ten years I can live on the money I have made, and then I'll go to Roumania and get myself an order. And I may—note well that I say *may*— end my days as a count.

JULIA. Splendid, splendid!

JEAN. Yes, in Roumania the title of count can be had for cash, and so you'll be a countess after all. My countess!

JULIA. What do I care about all I now cast behind me! Tell me that you love me: otherwise—yes, what am I otherwise?

JEAN. I will tell you so a thousand times—later. But not here. And above all, no sentimentality, or everything will be lost. We must look at the matter in cold blood, like sensible people. [Takes out a cigar, cuts of the point, and lights it] Sit down there now, and I'll sit here, and then we'll talk as if nothing had happened.

JULIA. [In despair] Good Lord! Have you then no feelings at all?

JEAN. I? No one is more full of feeling than I am. But I know how to control myself.

JULIA. A while ago you kissed my shoe—and now!

JEAN. [Severely] Yes, that was then. Now we have other things to think of.

JULIA. Don't speak harshly to me!

JEAN. No, but sensibly. One folly has been committed—don't let us commit any more! The count may be here at any moment, and before he comes our fate must be settled. What do you think of my plans for the future? Do you approve of them?

JULIA. They seem acceptable, on the whole. But there is one question: a big undertaking of that kind will require a big capital have you got it?

JEAN. [Chewing his cigar] I? Of course! I have my expert knowledge, my vast experience, my familiarity with several languages. That's the very best kind of capital, I should say.

JULIA. But it won't buy you a railroad ticket even.

JEAN. That's true enough. And that is just why I am looking for a backer to advance the needful cash.

JULIA. Where could you get one all of a sudden?

JEAN. It's for you to find him if you want to become my partner.

JULIA. I cannot do it, and I have nothing myself. [Pause.]

JEAN. Well, then that's off—

JULIA. And——

JEAN. Everything remains as before.

JULIA. Do you think I am going to stay under this roof as your concubine? Do you think I'll let the people point their fingers at me? Do you think I can look my father in the face after this? No, take me away from here, from all this humiliation and disgrace!— Oh, what have I done? My God, my God! [Breaks into tears.]

JEAN. So we have got around to that tune now!—What you have done? Nothing but what many others have done before you.

JULIA. [Crying hysterically] And now you're despising me!—I'm falling, I'm falling!

JEAN. Fall down to me, and I'll lift you up again afterwards.

JULIA. What horrible power drew me to you? Was it the attraction which the strong exercises on the weak—the one who is rising on one who is falling? Or was it love? This love! Do you know what love is?

JEAN. I? Well, I should say so! Don't you think I have been there before?

JULIA. Oh, the language you use, and the thoughts you think!

JEAN. Well, that's the way I was brought up, and that's the way I am. Don't get nerves now and play the exquisite, for now one of us is just as good as the other. Look here, my girl, let me treat you to a glass of something superfine. [He opens the table-drawer, takes out the wine bottle and fills up two glasses that have already been used.]

JULIA. Where did you get that wine?

JEAN. In the cellar.

JULIA. My father's Burgundy!

JEAN. Well, isn't it good enough for the son-in-law?

JULIA. And I am drinking beer—I!

JEAN. It shows merely that I have better taste than you.

JULIA. Thief!

JEAN. Do you mean to tell on me?

JULIA. Oh, oh! The accomplice of a house thief! Have I been drunk, or have I been dreaming all this night? Midsummer Eve! The feast of innocent games——

JEAN. Innocent—hm!

JULIA. [Walking back and forth] Can there be another human being on earth so unhappy as I am at this moment'

JEAN. But why should you be? After such a conquest? Think of Christine in there. Don't you think she has feelings also?

JULIA. I thought so a while ago, but I don't think so any longer. No, a menial is a menial—

JEAN. And a whore a whore!

JULIA. [On her knees, with folded hands] O God in heaven, make an end of this wretched life! Take me out of the filth into which I am sinking! Save me! Save me!

JEAN. I cannot deny that I feel sorry for you. When I was lying among the onions and saw you up there among the roses—I'll tell you now—I had the same nasty thoughts that all boys have.

JULIA. And you who wanted to die for my sake!

JEAN. Among the oats. That was nothing but talk.

JULIA. Lies in other words!

JEAN. [Beginning to feel sleepy] Just about. I think I read the story in a paper, and it was about a chimney-sweep who crawled into a wood-box full of lilacs because a girl had brought suit against him for not supporting her kid——

JULIA. So that's the sort you are—

JEAN. Well, I had to think of something—for it's the high-faluting stuff that the women bite on.

JULIA. Scoundrel!

JEAN. Rot!

JULIA. And now you have seen the back of the hawk—

JEAN. Well, I don't know—

JULIA. And I was to be the first branch—

JEAN. But the branch was rotten—

JULIA. I was to be the sign in front of the hotel—

JEAN. And I the hotel—

JULIA. Sit at your counter, and lure your customers, and doctor your bills—

JEAN. No, that I should have done myself—

JULIA. That a human soul can be so steeped in dirt!

JEAN. Well, wash it off!

JULIA. You lackey, you menial, stand up when I talk to you!

JEAN. You lackey-love, you mistress of a menial—shut up and get out of here! You're the right one to come and tell me that I am vulgar. People of my kind would never in their lives act as vulgarly as you have acted to-night. Do you think any servant girl would go for a man as you did? Did you ever see a girl of my class throw herself at anybody in that way? I have never seen the like of it except among beasts and prostitutes.

JULIA. [Crushed] That's right: strike me, step on me—I haven't deserved any better! I am a wretched creature. But help me! Help me out of this, if there be any way to do so!

JEAN. [In a milder tone] I don't want to lower myself by a denial of my share in the honour of seducing. But do you think a person in my place would have dared to raise his eyes to you, if the invitation to do so had not come from yourself? I am still sitting here in a state of utter surprise—

JULIA. And pride—

JEAN. Yes, why not? Although I must confess that the victory was too easy to bring with it any real intoxication.

JULIA. Strike me some more!

JEAN. [Rising] No! Forgive me instead what I have been saying. I don't want to strike one who is disarmed, and least of all a lady. On one hand I cannot deny that it has given me pleasure to discover that what has dazzled us below is nothing but cat-gold; that the hawk is simply grey on the back also; that there is powder on the tender cheek; that there may be black borders on the polished nails; and that the handkerchief may be dirty, although it smells of perfume. But on the other hand it hurts me to have discovered that what I was striving to reach is neither better nor more genuine. It hurts me to see you sinking so low that you are far beneath your own cook—it hurts me as it hurts to see the Fall flowers beaten down by the rain and turned into mud.

JULIA. You speak as if you were already above me?

JEAN. Well, so I am. Don't you see: I could have made a countess of you, but you could never make me a count.

JULIA. But I am born of a count, and that's more than you can ever achieve.

JEAN. That's true. But I might be the father of counts—if—

JULIA. But you are a thief—and I am not.

JEAN. Thief is not the worst. There are other kinds still farther down. And then, when I serve in a house, I regard myself in a sense as a member of the family, as a child of the house, and you don't call it theft when children pick a few of the berries that load down the vines. [His passion is aroused once more] Miss Julia, you are a magnificent woman, and far too good for one like me. You were swept along by a spell of intoxication, and now you want to cover up your mistake by making yourself believe that you are in love with me. Well, you are not, unless possibly my looks might tempt you——in which case your love is no better than mine. I could never rest satisfied with having you care for nothing in me but the mere animal, and your love I can never win.

JULIA. Are you so sure of that?

JEAN. You mean to say that it might be possible? That I might love you: yes, without doubt—for you are beautiful, refined, [goes up to her and takes hold of her hand] educated, charming when you want to be so, and it is not likely that the flame will ever burn out in a man who has once been set of fire by you. [Puts his arm around her waist] You are like burnt wine with strong spices in it, and one of your kisses—

[He tries to lead her away, but she frees herself gently from his hold.]

JULIA. Leave me alone! In that way you cannot win me.

JEAN. How then?—Not in that way! Not by caresses and sweet words! Not by thought for the future, by escape from disgrace! How then?

JULIA. How? How? I don't know—Not at all! I hate you as I hate rats, but I cannot escape from you!

JEAN. Escape with me!

JULIA. [Straightening up] Escape? Yes, we must escape!—But I am so tired. Give me a glass of wine.

[JEAN pours out wine.]

JULIA. [Looks at her watch] But we must have a talk first. We have still some time left. [Empties her glass and holds it out for more.]

JEAN. Don't drink so much. It will go to your head.

JULIA. What difference would that make?

JEAN. What difference would it make? It's vulgar to get drunk—What was it you wanted to tell me?

JULIA. We must get away. But first we must have a talk—that is, I must talk, for so far you have done all the talking. You have told me about your life. Now I must tell you about mine, so that we know each other right to the bottom before we begin the journey together.

JEAN. One moment, pardon me! Think first, so that you don't regret it afterwards, when you have already given up the secrets of your life.

JULIA. Are you not my friend?

JEAN. Yes, at times—but don't rely on me.

JULIA. You only talk like that—and besides, my secrets are known to everybody. You see, my mother was not of noble birth, but came of quite plain people. She was brought up in the ideas of her time about equality, and woman's independence, and that kind of thing. And she had a decided aversion to marriage. Therefore, when my father proposed to her, she said she wouldn't marry him—and then she did it just the same. I came into the world—against my mother's wish, I have come to think. Then my mother wanted to bring me up in a perfectly natural state, and at the same time I was to learn everything that a boy is taught, so that I might prove that a woman is just as good as a man. I was dressed as a boy, and was taught how to handle a horse, but could have nothing to do with the cows. I had to groom and harness and go hunting on horseback. I was even forced to learn something about agriculture. And all over the estate men were set to do women's work, and women to do men's—with the result that everything went to pieces and we became the laughing-stock of the whole neighbourhood. At last my father must have recovered from the spell cast over him, for he rebelled, and everything was changed to suit his own ideas. My mother was taken sick—what kind of sickness it was I don't know, but she fell often into convulsions, and she used to hide herself in the garret or in the garden, and sometimes she stayed out all night. Then came the big fire, of which you have heard. The house, the stable, and the barn were burned down, and this under circumstances which made it look as if the fire had been set on purpose. For the disaster occurred the day after our insurance expired, and the money sent for renewal of the policy had been delayed by the messenger's carelessness, so that it came too late. [She fills her glass again and drinks.]

JEAN. Don't drink any more.

JULIA. Oh, what does it matter!—We were without a roof over our heads and had to sleep in the carriages. My father didn't know where to get money for the rebuilding of the house. Then my mother suggested that he try to borrow from a childhood friend of hers, a brick manufacturer living not far from here. My father got the loan, but was not permitted to pay any interest, which astonished him. And so the house was built up again. [Drinks again] Do you know who set fire to the house?

JEAN. Her ladyship, your mother!

JULIA. Do you know who the brick manufacturer was?

JEAN. Your mother's lover?

JULIA. Do you know to whom the money belonged?

JEAN. Wait a minute—no, that I don't know.

JULIA. To my mother.

JEAN. In other words, to the count, if there was no settlement.

JULIA. There was no settlement. My mother possessed a small fortune of her own which she did not want to leave in my father's control, so she invested it with—her friend.

JEAN. Who copped it.

JULIA. Exactly! He kept it. All this came to my father's knowledge. He couldn't bring suit; he couldn't pay his wife's lover; he couldn't prove that it was his wife's money. That was my mother's revenge because he had made himself master in his own house. At that time he came near shooting himself—it was even rumoured that he had tried and failed. But he took a new lease of life, and my mother had to pay for what she had done. I can tell you that those were five years I'll never forget! My sympathies were with my father, but I took my mother's side because I was not aware of the true circumstances. From her I learned to suspect and hate men—for she hated the whole sex, as you have probably heard—and I promised her on my oath that I would never become a man's slave.

JEAN. And so you became engaged to the County Attorney.

JULIA. Yes, in order that he should be my slave.

JEAN. And he didn't want to?

JULIA. Oh, he wanted, but I wouldn't let him. I got tired of him.

JEAN. Yes, I saw it—in the stable-yard.

JULIA. What did you see?

JEAN. Just that—how he broke the engagement.

JULIA. That's a lie! It was I who broke it. Did he say he did it, the scoundrel?

JEAN. Oh, he was no scoundrel, I guess. So you hate men, Miss Julia?

JULIA. Yes! Most of the time. But now and then—when the weakness comes over me—oh, what shame!

JEAN. And you hate me too?

JULIA. Beyond measure! I should like to kill you like a wild beast—

JEAN. As you make haste to shoot a mad dog. Is that right?

JULIA. That's right!

JEAN. But now there is nothing to shoot with—and there is no dog. What are we to do then?

JULIA. Go abroad.

JEAN. In order to plague each other to death?

JULIA. No-in order to enjoy ourselves: a couple of days, a week, as long as enjoyment is possible. And then—die!

JEAN. Die? How silly! Then I think it's much better to start a hotel.

JULIA. [Without listening to JEAN]—At Lake Como, where the sun is always shining, and the laurels stand green at Christmas, and the oranges are glowing.

JEAN. Lake Como is a rainy hole, and I could see no oranges except in the groceries. But it is a good place for tourists, as it has a lot of villas that can be rented to loving couples, and that's a profitable business—do you know why? Because they take a lease for six months—and then they leave after three weeks.

JULIA. [Naïvely] Why after three weeks?

JEAN. Because they quarrel, of course. But the rent has to be paid just the same. And then you can rent the house again. And that way it goes on all the time, for there is plenty of love—even if it doesn't last long.

JULIA. You don't want to die with me?

JEAN. I don't want to die at all. Both because I am fond of living, and because I regard suicide as a crime against the Providence which has bestowed life on us.

JULIA. Do you mean to say that you believe in God?

JEAN. Of course, I do. And I go to church every other Sunday. Frankly speaking, now I am tired of all this, and now I am going to bed.

JULIA. So! And you think that will be enough for me? Do you know what you owe a woman that you have spoiled?

JEAN. [Takes out his purse and throws a silver coin on the table] You're welcome! I don't want to be in anybody's debt.

JULIA. [Pretending not to notice the insult] Do you know what the law provides—

JEAN. Unfortunately the law provides no punishment for a woman who seduces a man.

JULIA. [As before] Can you think of any escape except by our going abroad and getting married, and then getting a divorce?

JEAN. Suppose I refuse to enter into this *mésaillance*?

JULIA. *Mésaillance*—

JEAN. Yes, for me. You see, I have better ancestry than you, for nobody in my family was ever guilty of arson.

JULIA. How do you know?

JEAN. Well, nothing is known to the contrary, for we keep no Pedigrees—except in the police bureau. But I have read about your pedigree in a book that was lying on the drawing-room table. Do you know who was your first ancestor? A miller who let his wife sleep with the king one night during the war with Denmark. I have no such ancestry. I have none at all, but I can become an ancestor myself.

JULIA. That's what I get for unburdening my heart to one not worthy of it; for sacrificing my family's honour—

JEAN. Dishonour! Well, what was it I told you? You shouldn't drink, for then you talk. And you must not talk!

JULIA. Oh, how I regret what I have done! How I regret it! If at least you loved me!

JEAN. For the last time: what do you mean? Am I to weep? Am I to jump over your whip? Am I to kiss you, and lure you down to Lake Como for three weeks, and so on? What am I to do? What do you expect? This is getting to be rather painful! But that's what comes from getting mixed up with women. Miss Julia! I see that you are unhappy; I know that you are suffering; but I cannot understand you. We never carry on like that. There is never any hatred between us. Love is to us a play, and we play at it when our work leaves us time to do so. But we have not the time to do so all day and all night, as you have. I believe you are sick—I am sure you are sick.

JULIA. You should be good to me—and now you speak like a human being.

JEAN. All right, but be human yourself. You spit on me, and then you won't let me wipe myself—on you!

JULIA. Help me, help me! Tell me only what I am to do—where I am to turn?

JEAN. O Lord, if I only knew that myself!

JULIA. I have been exasperated, I have been mad, but there ought to be some way of saving myself.

JEAN. Stay right here and keep quiet. Nobody knows anything.

JULIA. Impossible! The people know, and Christine knows.

JEAN. They don't know, and they would never believe it possible.

JULIA. [Hesitating] But-it might happen again.

JEAN. That's true.

JULIA. And the results?

JEAN. [Frightened] The results! Where was my head when I didn't think of that! Well, then there is only one thing to do—you must leave. At once! I can't go with you, for then everything would be lost, so you must go alone—abroad—anywhere!

JULIA. Alone? Where?—I can't do it.

JEAN. You must! And before the count gets back. If you stay, then you know what will happen. Once on the wrong path, one wants to keep on, as the harm is done anyhow. Then one grows more and more reckless—and at last it all comes out. So you must get away! Then you can write to the count and tell him everything, except that it was me. And he would never guess it. Nor do I think he would be very anxious to find out.

JULIA. I'll go if you come with me.

JEAN. Are you stark mad, woman? Miss Julia to run away with her valet! It would be in the papers in another day, and the count could never survive it.

JULIA. I can't leave! I can't stay! Help me! I am so tired, so fearfully tired. Give me orders! Set me going, for I can no longer think, no longer act—

JEAN. Do you see now what good-for-nothings you are! Why do you strut and turn up your noses as if you were the lords of creation? Well, I am going to give you orders. Go up and dress. Get some travelling money, and then come back again.

JULIA: [In an undertone] Come up with me!

JEAN. To your room? Now you're crazy again! [Hesitates a moment] No, you must go at once! [Takes her by the hand and leads her out.]

JULIA. [On her way out] Can't you speak kindly to me, Jean?

JEAN. An order must always sound unkind. Now you can find out how it feels!

[JULIA goes out.]

[JEAN, alone, draws a sigh of relief; sits down at the table; takes out a note-book and a pencil; figures aloud from time to time; dumb play until CHRISTINE enters dressed for church; she has a false shirt front and a white tie in one of her hands.]

CHRISTINE. Goodness gracious, how the place looks! What have you been up to anyhow?

JEAN. Oh, it was Miss Julia who dragged in the people. Have you been sleeping so hard that you didn't hear anything at all?

CHRISTINE. I have been sleeping like a log.

JEAN. And dressed for church already?

CHRISTINE. Yes, didn't you promise to come with me to communion to-day?

JEAN. Oh, yes, I remember now. And there you've got the finery. Well, come on with it. [Sits down; CHRISTINE helps him to put on the shirt front and the white tie.]

[Pause.]

JEAN. [Sleepily] What's the text to-day?

CHRISTINE. Oh, about John the Baptist beheaded, I guess.

JEAN. That's going to be a long story, I'm sure. My, but you choke me! Oh, I'm so sleepy, so sleepy!

CHRISTINE. Well, what has been keeping you up all night? Why, man, you're just green in the face!

JEAN. I have been sitting here talking with Miss Julia.

CHRISTINE. She hasn't an idea of what's proper, that creature!

[Pause.]

JEAN. Say, Christine.

CHRISTINE. Well?

JEAN. Isn't it funny anyhow, when you come to think of it? Her!

CHRISTINE. What is it that's funny?

JEAN. Everything!

[Pause.]

CHRISTINE. [Seeing the glasses on the table that are only half-emptied] So you've been drinking together also?

JEAN. Yes.

CHRISTINE. Shame on you! Look me in the eye!

JEAN. Yes.

CHRISTINE. Is it possible? Is it possible?

JEAN. [After a moment's thought] Yes, it is!

CHRISTINE. Ugh! That's worse than I could ever have believed. It's awful!

JEAN. You are not jealous of her, are you?

CHRISTINE. No, not of her. Had it been Clara or Sophie, then I'd have scratched your eyes out. Yes, that's the way I feel about it, and I can't tell why. Oh my, but that was nasty!

JEAN. Are you mad at her then?

CHRISTINE. No, but at you! It was wrong of you, very wrong! Poor girl! No, I tell you, I don't want to stay in this house any longer, with people for whom it is impossible to have any respect.

JEAN. Why should you have any respect for them?

CHRISTINE. And you who are such a smarty can't tell that! You wouldn't serve people who don't act decently, would you? It's to lower oneself, I think.

JEAN. Yes, but it ought to be a consolation to us that they are not a bit better than we.

CHRISTINE. No, I don't think so. For if they're no better, then it's no use trying to get up to them. And just think of the count! Think of him who has had so much sorrow in his day! No, I don't want to stay any longer in this house— And with a fellow like you, too. If it had been the county attorney—if it had only been some one of her own sort—

JEAN. Now look here!

CHRISTINE. Yes, yes! You're all right in your way, but there's after all some difference between one kind of people and another—— No, but this is something I'll never get over!—And the young lady who was so proud, and so tart to the men, that you couldn't believe she would ever let one come near her—and such a one at that! And she who wanted to have poor Diana shot because she had been running around with the gate-keeper's pug!—Well, I declare!—But I won't stay here any longer, and next October I get out of here.

JEAN. And then?

CHRISTINE. Well, as we've come to talk of that now, perhaps it would be just as well if you looked for something, seeing that we're going to get married after all.

JEAN. Well, what could I look for? As a married man I couldn't get a place like this.

CHRISTINE. No, I understand that. But you could get a job as a janitor, or maybe as a messenger in some government bureau. Of course, the public loaf is always short in weight, but it comes steady, and then there is a pension for the widow and the children—

JEAN. [Making a face] That's good and well, but it isn't my style to think of dying all at once for the sake of wife and children. I must say that my plans have been looking toward something better than that kind of thing.

CHRISTINE. Your plans, yes—but you've got obligations also, and those you had better keep in mind!

JEAN. Now don't you get my dander up by talking of obligations! I know what I've got to do anyhow. [Listening for some sound on the outside] However, we've plenty of time to think of all this. Go in now and get ready, and then we'll go to church.

CHRISTINE. Who is walking around up there?

JEAN. I don't know, unless it be Clara.

CHRISTINE. [Going out] It can't be the count, do you think, who's come home without anybody hearing him?

JEAN. [Scared] The count? No, that isn't possible, for then he would have rung for me.

CHRISTINE. [As she goes out] Well, God help us all! Never have I seen the like of it!

[The sun has risen and is shining on the tree tops in the park. The light changes gradually until it comes slantingly in through the windows. JEAN goes to the door and gives a signal.]

JULIA. [Enters in travelling dress and carrying a small birdcage covered up with a towel; this she places on a chair] Now I am ready.

JEAN. Hush! Christine is awake.

JULIA. [Showing extreme nervousness during the following scene] Did she suspect anything?

JEAN. She knows nothing at all. But, my heavens, how you look!

JULIA. How do I look?

JEAN. You're as pale as a corpse, and—pardon me, but your face is dirty.

JULIA. Let me wash it then—Now! [She goes over to the washstand and washes her face and hands] Give me a towel—Oh!—That's the sun rising!

JEAN. And then the ogre bursts.

JULIA. Yes, ogres and trolls were abroad last night!—But listen, Jean. Come with me, for now I have the money.

JEAN. [Doubtfully] Enough?

JULIA. Enough to start with. Come with me, for I cannot travel alone to-day. Think of it—Midsummer Day, on a stuffy train, jammed with people who stare at you—and standing still at stations when you want to fly. No, I cannot! I cannot! And then the memories will come: childhood memories of Midsummer Days, when the inside of the church was turned into a green forest—birches and lilacs; the dinner at the festive table with relatives and friends; the afternoon in the park, with dancing and music, flowers and games! Oh, you may run and run, but your memories are in the baggage-car, and with them remorse and repentance!

JEAN. I'll go with you-but at once, before it's too late. This very moment!

JULIA. Well, get dressed then. [Picks up the cage.]

JEAN. But no baggage! That would only give us away.

JULIA. No, nothing at all! Only what we can take with us in the car.

JEAN. [Has taken down his hat] What have you got there? What is it?

JULIA. It's only my finch. I can't leave it behind.

JEAN. Did you ever! Dragging a bird-cage along with us! You must be raving mad! Drop the cage!

JULIA. The only thing I take with me from my home! The only living creature that loves me since Diana deserted me! Don't be cruel! Let me take it along!

JEAN. Drop the cage, I tell you! And don't talk so loud—Christine can hear us.

JULIA. No, I won't let it fall into strange hands. I'd rather have you kill it!

JEAN. Well, give it to me, and I'll wring its neck.

JULIA. Yes, but don't hurt it. Don't—no, I cannot!

JEAN. Let me—I can!

JULIA. [Takes the bird out of the cage and kisses it] Oh, my little birdie, must it die and go away from its mistress!

JEAN. Don't make a scene, please. Don't you know it's a question of your life, of your future? Come, quick! [Snatches the bird away from her, carries it to the chopping block and picks up an axe. MISS JULIA turns away.]

JEAN. You should have learned how to kill chickens instead of shooting with a revolver—[brings down the axe]—then you wouldn't have fainted for a drop of blood.

JULIA. [Screaming] Kill me too! Kill me! You who can take the life of an innocent creature without turning a hair! Oh, I hate and despise you! There is blood between us! Cursed be the hour when I first met you! Cursed be the hour when I came to life in my mother's womb!

JEAN. Well, what's the use of all that cursing? Come on!

JULIA. [Approaching the chopping-block as if drawn to it against her will] No, I don't want to go yet. I cannot——I must see—Hush! There's a carriage coming up the road. [Listening without taking her eyes of the block and the axe] You think I cannot stand the sight of blood. You think I am as weak as that— oh, I should like to see your blood, your brains, on that block there. I should like to see your whole sex swimming in blood like that thing there. I think I could drink out of your skull, and bathe my feet in your open breast, and eat your heart from the spit!—You think I am weak; you think I love you because the fruit of my womb was yearning for your seed; you think I want to carry your offspring under my heart and nourish it with my blood—bear your children and take your name! Tell me, you, what are you called anyhow? I have never heard your family name—and maybe you haven't any. I should become Mrs. "Hovel," or Mrs. "Backyard"—you dog there, that's wearing my collar; you lackey with my coat of arms on your buttons— and I should share with my cook, and be the rival of my own servant. Oh! Oh! Oh!—You think I am a coward and want to run away! No, now I'll stay—and let the lightning strike! My father will come home—will find his chiffonier opened—the money gone! Then he'll ring—twice for the valet—and then he'll send for the sheriff—and then I shall tell everything! Everything! Oh, but it will be good to get an end to it—if it only be the end! And then his heart will break, and he dies!—So there will be an end to all of us—and all will be quiet—peace—eternal rest!—And then the coat of arms will be shattered on the coffin—and the count's line will be wiped out— but the lackey's line goes on in the orphan asylum—wins laurels in the gutter, and ends in jail.

JEAN. There spoke the royal blood! Bravo, Miss Julia! Now you put the miller back in his sack!

[CHRISTINE enters dressed for church and carrying n hymn-book in her hand.]

JULIA. [Hurries up to her and throws herself into her arms ax if seeking protection] Help me, Christine! Help me against this man!

CHRISTINE. [Unmoved and cold] What kind of performance is this on the Sabbath morning? [Catches sight of the chopping-block] My, what a mess you have made!—What's the meaning of all this? And the way you shout and carry on!

JULIA. You are a woman, Christine, and you are my friend. Beware of that scoundrel!

JEAN. [A little shy and embarrassed] While the ladies are discussing I'll get myself a shave. [Slinks out to the right.]

JULIA. You must understand me, and you must listen to me.

CHRISTINE. No, really, I don't understand this kind of trolloping. Where are you going in your travelling-dress—and he with his hat on—what?—What?

JULIA. Listen, Christine, listen, and I'll tell you everything—

CHRISTINE. I don't want to know anything—

JULIA. You must listen to me—

CHRISTINE. What is it about? Is it about this nonsense with Jean? Well, I don't care about it at all, for it's none of my business. But if you're planning to get him away with you, we'll put a stop to that!

JULIA. [Extremely nervous] Please try to be quiet, Christine, and listen to me. I cannot stay here, and Jean cannot stay here—and so we must leave—-

CHRISTINE. Hm, hm!

JULIA. [Brightening. up] But now I have got an idea, you know. Suppose all three of us should leave—go abroad—go to Switzerland and start a hotel together—I have money, you know—and Jean and I could run the whole thing— and you, I thought, could take charge of the kitchen—Wouldn't that be fine!—Say yes, now! And come along with us! Then everything is fixed!—Oh, say yes!

[She puts her arms around CHRISTINE and pats her.]

CHRISTINE. [Coldly and thoughtfully] Hm, hm!

JULIA. [Presto tempo] You have never travelled, Christine—you must get out and have a look at the world. You cannot imagine what fun it is to travel on a train—constantly new people—new countries—- and then we get to Hamburg and take in the Zoological Gardens in passing—that's what you like—and then we go to the theatres and to the opera—and when we get to Munich, there, you know, we have a lot of museums, where they keep Rubens and Raphael and all those big painters, you know—Haven't you heard of Munich, where King Louis used to live—the king, you know, that went mad—And then we'll have a look at his castle—he has still some castles that are furnished just as in a fairy tale—and from there it isn't very far to Switzerland—and the Alps, you know—just think of the Alps, with snow on top of them in the middle of the summer—and there you have orange trees and laurels that are green all the year around—

[JEAN is seen in the right wing, sharpening his razor on a strop which he holds between his teeth and his left hand; he listens to the talk with a pleased mien and nods approval now and then.]

JULIA. [Tempo prestissimo] And then we get a hotel—and I sit in the office, while Jean is outside receiving tourists—and goes out marketing—and writes letters—That's a life for you—Then the train whistles, and the 'bus drives up, and it rings upstairs, and it rings in the restaurant—and then I make out the bills—and I am going to salt them, too—You can never imagine how timid tourists are when they come to pay their bills! And you—you will sit like a queen in the kitchen. Of course, you are not going to stand at the stove yourself. And you'll have to dress neatly and nicely in order to show yourself to people—and with your looks—yes, I am not flattering you—you'll catch a husband some fine day—some rich Englishman, you know-—for those fellows are so easy [slowing down] to catch—and then we grow rich—and we build us a villa at Lake Como—of course, it is raining a little in that place now and then—- but [limply] the sun must be shining sometimes—although it looks dark—and—then—or else we can go home again—and come back—here—- or some other place—

CHRISTINE. Tell me, Miss Julia, do you believe in all that yourself?

JULIA. [Crushed] Do I believe in it myself?

CHRISTINE. Yes.

JULIA. [Exhausted] I don't know: I believe no longer in anything. [She sinks down on the bench and drops her head between her arms on the table] Nothing! Nothing at all!

CHRISTINE. [Turns to the right, where JEAN is standing] So you were going to run away!

JEAN. [Abashed, puts the razor on the table] Run away? Well, that's putting it rather strong. You have heard what the young lady proposes, and though she is tired out now by being up all night, it's a proposition that can be put through all right.

CHRISTINE. Now you tell me: did you mean me to act as cook for that one there—?

JEAN. [Sharply] Will you please use decent language in speaking to your mistress! Do you understand?

CHRISTINE. Mistress!

JEAN. Yes!

CHRISTINE. Well, well! Listen to him!

JEAN. Yes, it would be better for you to listen a little more and talk a little less. Miss Julia is your mistress, and what makes you disrespectful to her now should snake you feel the same way about yourself.

CHRISTINE. Oh, I have always had enough respect for myself—

JEAN. To have none for others!

CHRISTINE. —not to go below my own station. You can't say that the count's cook has had anything to do with the groom or the swineherd. You can't say anything of the kind!

JEAN. Yes, it's your luck that you have had to do with a gentleman.

CHRISTINE. Yes, a gentleman who sells the oats out of the count's stable!

JEAN. What's that to you who get a commission on the groceries and bribes from the butcher?

CHRISTINE. What's that?

JEAN. And so you can't respect your master and mistress any longer! You—you!

CHRISTINE. Are you coming with me to church? I think you need a good sermon on top of such a deed.

JEAN. No, I am not going to church to-day. You can go by yourself and confess your own deeds.

CHRISTINE. Yes, I'll do that, and I'll bring back enough forgiveness to cover you also. The Saviour suffered and died on the cross for all our sins, and if we go to him with a believing heart and a repentant mind, he'll take all our guilt on himself.

JULIA. Do you believe that, Christine?

CHRISTINE. It is my living belief, as sure as I stand here, and the faith of my childhood which I have kept since I was young, Miss Julia. And where sin abounds, grace abounds too.

JULIA. Oh, if I had your faith! Oh, if—

CHRISTINE. Yes, but you don't get it without the special grace of God, and that is not bestowed on everybody—

JULIA. On whom is it bestowed then?

CHRISTINE. That's just the great secret of the work of grace, Miss Julia, and the Lord has no regard for persons, but there those that are last shall be the foremost—

JULIA. Yes, but that means he has regard for those that are last.

CHRISTINE. [Going right on] —and it is easier for a camel to go through a needle's eye than for a rich man to get into heaven. That's the way it is, Miss Julia. Now I am going, however—alone— and as I pass by, I'll tell the stableman not to let out the horses if anybody should like to get away before the count comes home. Good-bye! [Goes out.]

JEAN. Well, ain't she a devil!—And all this for the sake of a finch!

JULIA. [Apathetically] Never mind the finch!—Can you see any way out of this, any way to end it?

JEAN. [Ponders] No!

JULIA. What would you do in my place?

JEAN. In your place? Let me see. As one of gentle birth, as a woman, as one who has—fallen. I don't know—yes, I do know!

JULIA. [Picking up the razor with a significant gesture] Like this?

JEAN. Yes!—But please observe that I myself wouldn't do it, for there is a difference between us.

JULIA. Because you are a man and I a woman? What is the difference?

JEAN. It is the same—as—that between man and woman.

JULIA. [With the razor in her hand] I want to, but I cannot!—My father couldn't either, that time he should have done it.

JEAN. No, he should not have done it, for he had to get his revenge first.

JULIA. And now it is my mother's turn to revenge herself again, through me.

JEAN. Have you not loved your father, Miss Julia?

JULIA. Yes, immensely, but I must have hated him, too. I think I must have been doing so without being aware of it. But he was the one who reared me in contempt for my own sex—half woman and half man! Whose fault is it, this that has happened? My father's—my mother's—my own? My own? Why, I have nothing that is my own. I haven't a thought that didn't come from my father; not a passion that didn't come from my mother; and now this last—this about all human creatures being equal—I got that from him, my fiancé—whom I call a scoundrel for that reason! How can it be my own fault? To put the blame on Jesus, as Christine does—no, I am too proud for that, and know too much—thanks to my father's teachings—And that about a rich person not getting into heaven, it's just a lie, and Christine, who has money in the savings-bank, wouldn't get in anyhow. Whose is the fault?—What does it matter whose it is? For just the same I am the one who must bear the guilt and the results—

JEAN. Yes, but—

[Two sharp strokes are rung on the bell. MISS JULIA leaps to her feet. JEAN changes his coat.]

JEAN. The count is back. Think if Christine— [Goes to the speaking-tube, knocks on it, and listens.]

JULIA. Now he has been to the chiffonier!

JEAN. It is Jean, your lordship! [Listening again, the spectators being unable to hear what the count says] Yes, your lordship! [Listening] Yes, your lordship! At once! [Listening] In a minute, your lordship! [Listening] Yes, yes! In half an hour!

JULIA. [With intense concern] What did he say? Lord Jesus, what did he say?

JEAN. He called for his boots and wanted his coffee in half an hour.

JULIA. In half an hour then! Oh, I am so tired. I can't do anything; can't repent, can't run away, can't stay, can't live—— can't die! Help me now! Command me, and I'll obey you like a dog! Do me this last favour—save my honour, and save his name! You know what my will ought to do, and what it cannot do—now give me your will, and make me do it!

JEAN. I don't know why—but now I can't either—I don't understand—- It is just as if this coat here made a—I cannot command you—and now, since I've heard the count's voice—now—I can't quite explain it—but—Oh, that damned menial is back in my spine again. I believe if the count should come down here, and if he should tell me to cut my own throat—I'd do it on the spot!

JULIA. Make believe that you are he, and that I am you! You did some fine acting when you were on your knees before me—then you were the nobleman—or—have you ever been to a show and seen one who could hypnotize people?

[JEAN makes a sign of assent.]

JULIA. He says to his subject: get the broom. And the man gets it. He says: sweep. And the man sweeps.

JEAN. But then the other person must be asleep.

JULIA. [Ecstatically] I am asleep already—there is nothing in the whole room but a lot of smoke—and you look like a stove—that looks like a man in black clothes and a high hat—and your eyes glow like coals when the fire is going out—and your face is a lump of white ashes. [The sunlight has reached the floor and is now falling on JEAN] How warm and nice it is! [She rubs her hands as if warming them before a fire.] And so light—and so peaceful!

JEAN. [Takes the razor and puts it in her hand] There's the broom! Go now, while it is light—to the barn—and— [Whispers something in her ear.]

JULIA. [Awake] Thank you! Now I shall have rest! But tell me first—- that the foremost also receive the gift of grace. Say it, even if you don't believe it.

JEAN. The foremost? No, I can't do that!—But wait—Miss Julia—I know! You are no longer among the foremost—now when you are among the—last!

JULIA. That's right. I am among the last of all: I am the very last. Oh!—But now I cannot go—Tell me once more that I must go!

JEAN. No, now I can't do it either. I cannot!

JULIA. And those that are foremost shall be the last.

JEAN. Don't think, don't think! Why, you are taking away my strength, too, so that I become a coward—What? I thought I saw the bell moving!—To be that scared of a bell! Yes, but it isn't only the bell—there is somebody behind it—a hand that makes it move—- and something else that makes the hand move-but if you cover up your ears—just cover up your ears! Then it rings worse than ever! Rings and rings, until you answer it—and then it's too late—then comes the sheriff—and then—

[Two quick rings from the bell.]

JEAN. [Shrinks together; then he straightens himself up] It's horrid! But there's no other end to it!—Go!

[JULIA goes firmly out through the door.]

(Curtain.)

THE STRONGER

INTRODUCTION

OF Strindberg's dramatic works the briefest is "The Stronger." He called it a "scene." It is a mere incident—what is called a "sketch" on our vaudeville stage, and what the French so aptly have named a "quart d'heure." And one of the two figures in the cast remains silent throughout the action, thus turning the little play practically into a monologue. Yet it has all the dramatic intensity which we have come to look upon as one of the main characteristics of Strindberg's work for the stage. It is quivering with mental conflict, and because of this conflict human destinies may be seen to change while we are watching. Three life stories are laid bare during the few minutes we are listening to the seemingly aimless, yet so ominous, chatter of *Mrs. X.*—and when she sallies forth at last, triumphant in her sense of possession, we know as much about her, her husband, and her rival, as if we had been reading a three-volume novel about them.

Small as it is, the part of *Mrs. X.* would befit a "star," but an actress of genius and discernment might prefer the dumb part of *Miss Y.* One thing is certain: that the latter character has few equals in its demand on the performer's tact and skill and imagination. This wordless opponent of *Mrs. X.* is another of those vampire characters which Strindberg was so fond of drawing, and it is on her the limelight is directed with merciless persistency.

"The Stronger" was first published in 1890, as part of the collection of miscellaneous writings which their author named "Things Printed and Unprinted." The present English version was made by me some years ago—in the summer of 1906—when I first began to plan a Strindberg edition for this country. At that time it appeared in the literary supplement of the *New York Evening Post.*

THE STRONGER
A SCENE
1890

PERSONS

MRS. X., an actress, married.
MISS Y., an actress, unmarried.
THE STRONGER

SCENE

[A corner of a ladies' restaurant; two small tables of cast-iron, a sofa covered with red plush, and a few chairs.]

[MRS. X. enters dressed in hat and winter coat, and carrying a pretty Japanese basket on her arm.]

[MISS Y. has in front of her a partly emptied bottle of beer; she is reading an illustrated weekly, and every now and then she exchanges it for a new one.]

MRS. X. Well, how do, Millie! Here you are sitting on Christmas Eve as lonely as a poor bachelor.

[MISS Y. looks up from the paper for a moment, nods, and resumes her reading.]

MRS. X. Really, I feel sorry to find you like this—alone—alone in a restaurant, and on Christmas Eve of all times. It makes me as sad as when I saw a wedding party at Paris once in a restaurant—the bride was reading a comic paper and the groom was playing billiards with the witnesses. Ugh, when it begins that way, I thought, how will it end? Think of it, playing billiards on his wedding day! Yes, and you're going to say that she was reading a comic paper— that's a different case, my dear.

[A WAITRESS brings a cup of chocolate, places it before MRS. X., and disappears again.]

MRS. X. [Sips a few spoonfuls; opens the basket and displays a number of Christmas presents] See what I've bought for my tots. [Picks up a doll] What do you think of this? Lisa is to have it. She can roll her eyes and twist her head, do you see? Fine, is it not? And here's a cork pistol for Carl. [Loads the pistol and pops it at Miss Y.]

[MISS Y. starts as if frightened.]

MRS. X. Did I scare you? Why, you didn't fear I was going to shoot you, did you? Really, I didn't think you could believe that of me. If you were to shoot *me*—well, that wouldn't surprise me the least. I've got in your way once, and I know you'll never forget it—but I couldn't help it. You still think I intrigued you away from the Royal Theatre, and I didn't do anything of the kind— although you think so. But it doesn't matter what I say, of course— you believe it was I just the same. [Pulls out a pair of embroidered slippers] Well, these are for my hubby—tulips—I've embroidered them myself. Hm, I hate tulips—and he must have them on everything.

[MISS Y. looks up from the paper with an expression of mingled sarcasm and curiosity.]

MRS. X. [Puts a hand in each slipper] Just see what small feet Bob has. See? And you should see him walk—elegant! Of course, you've never seen him in slippers.

[MISS Y. laughs aloud.]

MRS. X. Look here—here he comes. [Makes the slippers walk across the table.]

[MISS Y. laughs again.]

MRS. X. Then he gets angry, and he stamps his foot just like this: "Blame that cook who can't learn how to make coffee." Or: "The idiot—now that girl has forgotten to fix my study lamp again." Then there is a draught through the floor and his feet get cold: "Gee, but it's freezing, and those blanked idiots don't even know enough to keep the house warm." [She rubs the sole of one slipper against the instep of the other.]

[MISS Y. breaks into prolonged laughter.]

MRS. X. And then he comes home and has to hunt for his slippers— Mary has pushed them under the bureau. Well, perhaps it is not right to be making fun of one's own husband. He's pretty good for all that—a real dear little hubby, that's what he is. You should have such a husband—what are you laughing at? Can't you tell? Then, you see, I know he is faithful. Yes, I know, for he has told me himself—what in the world makes you giggle like that? That nasty Betty tried to get him away from me while I was on the road—- can you think of anything more infamous? [Pause] But I'd have scratched the eyes out of her face, that's what I'd have done if I had been at home when she tried it. [Pause] I'm glad Bob told me all about it, so I didn't have to hear it first from somebody else. [Pause] And just think of it, Betty was not the only one! I don't know why it is, but all women seem to be crazy after my husband. It must be because they imagine his government position gives him something to say about the engagements. Perhaps you've tried it yourself—you may have set your traps for him, too? Yes, I don't trust you very far—but I know he never cared for you—and then I have been thinking you rather had a grudge against him.

[Pause. They look at each other in an embarrassed manner.]

MRS. X. Amèlia, spend the evening with us, won't you? Just to show that you are not angry—not with me, at least. I cannot tell exactly why, but it seems so awfully unpleasant to have you—you for an enemy. Perhaps because I got in your way that time [rallentando] or—I don't know—really, I don't know at all—

[Pause. MISS Y. gazes searchingly at MRS. X.]

MRS. X. [Thoughtfully] It was so peculiar, the way our acquaintance— why, I was afraid of you when I first met you; so afraid that I did not dare to let you out of sight. It didn't matter where I tried to go—I always found myself near you. I didn't have the courage to be your enemy—and so I became your friend. But there was always something discordant in the air when you called at our home, for I saw that my husband didn't like you—and it annoyed me just as it does when a dress won't fit. I tried my very best to make him appear friendly to you at least, but I couldn't move him—not until you were engaged. Then you two became such fast friends that it almost looked as if you had not dared to show your real feelings before, when it was not safe—and later—let me see, now! I didn't get jealous—strange, was it not? And I remember the baptism— you were acting as godmother, and I made him kiss you—and he did, but both of you looked terribly embarrassed—that is, I didn't think of it then—or afterwards, even—I never thought of it—till—*now*! [Rises impulsively] Why don't you say something? You have not uttered a single word all this time. You've just let me go on talking. You've been sitting there staring at me only, and your eyes have drawn out of me all these thoughts which were lying in me like silk in a cocoon—thoughts—bad thoughts maybe—let me think. Why did you break your engagement? Why have you never called on us afterward? Why don't you want to be with us to-night?

[MISS Y. makes a motion as if intending to speak.]

MRS. X. No, you don't need to say anything at all. All is clear to me now. So, that's the reason of it all. Yes, yes! Everything fits together now. Shame on you! I don't want to sit at the same table with you. [Moves her things to another table] That's why I must put those hateful tulips on his slippers—because you love them. [Throws the slippers on the floor] That's why we have to spend the summer in the mountains—because you can't bear the salt smell of the ocean; that's why my boy had to be called Eskil—because that was your father's name; that's why I had to wear your colour, and read your books, and eat your favourite dishes, and drink your drinks—this chocolate, for instance; that's why—great heavens!— it's terrible to think of it—it's terrible! Everything was forced on me by you—even your passions. Your soul bored itself into mine as a worm into an apple, and it ate and ate, and burrowed and burrowed, till nothing was left but the outside shell and a little black dust. I wanted to run away from you, but I couldn't. You were always on hand like a snake with your black eyes to charm me—I felt how my wings beat the air only to drag me down—I was in the water, with my feet tied together, and the harder I worked with my arms, the further down I went—down, down, till I sank to the bottom, where you lay in wait like a monster crab to catch me with your claws—and now I'm there! Shame on you! How I hate you, hate you, hate you! But you, you just sit there, silent and calm and indifferent, whether the moon is new or full; whether it's Christmas or mid-summer; whether other people are happy or unhappy. You are incapable of hatred, and you don't know how to love. As a cat in front of a mouse-hole, you are sitting there!—you can't drag your prey out, and you can't pursue it, but you can outwait it. Here you sit in this corner—do you know they've nicknamed it "the mouse-trap" on your account? Here you read the papers to see if anybody is in trouble, or if anybody is about to be discharged from the theatre. Here you watch your victims and calculate your chances and take your tributes. Poor Amèlia! Do you know, I pity you all the same, for I know you are unhappy—unhappy as one who has been wounded, and malicious because you are wounded. I ought to be angry with you, but really I can't—you are so small after all— and as to Bob, why that does not bother me in the least.

What does it matter to me anyhow? If you or somebody else taught me to drink chocolate—what of that? [Takes a spoonful of chocolate; then sententiously] They say chocolate is very wholesome. And if I have learned from you how to dress—*tant mieux*!—it has only given me a stronger hold on my husband—and you have lost where I have gained. Yes, judging by several signs, I think you have lost him already. Of course, you meant me to break with him—as you did, and as you are now regretting—but, you see, *I* never would do that. It won't do to be narrow-minded, you know. And why should I take only what nobody else wants? Perhaps, after all, I am the stronger now. You never got anything from me; you merely gave—and thus happened to me what happened to the thief—I had what you missed when you woke up. How explain in any other way that, in your hand, everything proved worthless and useless? You were never able to keep a man's love, in spite of your tulips and your passions—and I could; you could never learn the art of living from the books—as I learned it; you bore no little Eskil, although that was your father's name. And why do you keep silent always and everywhere— silent, ever silent? I used to think it was because you were so strong; and maybe the simple truth was you never had anything to say— because you were unable to-think! [Rises and picks up the slippers] I'm going home now—I'll take the tulips with me—your tulips. You couldn't learn anything from others; you couldn't bend and so you broke like a dry stem—and I didn't. Thank you, Amèlia, for all your instructions. I thank you that you have taught me how to love my husband. Now I'm going home—to him! [Exit.]

(Curtain.)

CREDITORS

INTRODUCTION

THIS is one of the three plays which Strindberg placed at the head of his dramatic production during the middle ultra-naturalistic period, the other two being "The Father" and "Miss Julia." It is, in many ways, one of the strongest he ever produced. Its rarely excelled unity of construction, its tremendous dramatic tension, and its wonderful psychological analysis combine to make it a masterpiece.

In Swedish its name is "Fordringsägare." This indefinite form may be either singular or plural, but it is rarely used except as a plural. And the play itself makes it perfectly clear that the proper translation of its title is "Creditors," for under this aspect appear both the former and the present husband of *Tekla*. One of the main objects of the play is to reveal her indebtedness first to one and then to the other of these men, while all the time she is posing as a person of original gifts.

I have little doubt that Strindberg, at the time he wrote this play—and bear in mind that this happened only a year before he finally decided to free himself from an impossible marriage by an appeal to the law—believed *Tekla* to be fairly representative of womanhood in general. The utter unreasonableness of such a view need hardly be pointed out, and I shall waste no time on it. A question more worthy of discussion is whether the figure of *Tekla* be true to life merely as the picture of a personality—as one out of numerous imaginable variations on a type decided not by sex but by faculties and qualities. And the same question may well be raised in regard to the two men, both of whom are evidently intended to win our sympathy: one as the victim of a fate stronger than himself, and the other as the conqueror of adverse and humiliating circumstances.

Personally, I am inclined to doubt whether a *Tekla* can be found in the flesh—and even if found, she might seem too exceptional to gain acceptance as a real individuality. It must be remembered, however, that, in spite of his avowed realism, Strindberg did not draw his men and women in the spirit generally designated as impressionistic; that is, with the idea that they might step straight from his pages into life and there win recognition as human beings of familiar aspect. His realism is always mixed with idealism; his figures are always "doctored," so to speak. And they have been thus treated in order to enable their creator to drive home the particular truth he is just then concerned with.

Consciously or unconsciously he sought to produce what may be designated as "pure cultures" of certain human qualities. But these he took great pains to arrange in their proper psychological settings, for mental and moral qualities, like everything else, run in groups that are more or less harmonious, if not exactly homogeneous. The man with a single quality, like Molière's *Harpagon*, was much too primitive and crude for Strindberg's art, as he himself rightly asserted in his preface to "Miss Julia." When he wanted to draw the genius of greed, so to speak, he did it by setting it in the midst of related qualities of a kind most likely to be attracted by it.

Tekla is such a "pure culture" of a group of naturally correlated mental and moral qualities and functions and tendencies—of a personality built up logically around a dominant central note. There are within all of us many personalities, some of which remain for ever potentialities. But it is conceivable that any one of them, under circumstances different from those in which we have been living, might have developed into its severely logical consequence—or, if you please, into a human being that would be held abnormal if actually encountered.

This is exactly what Strindberg seems to have done time and again, both in his middle and final periods, in his novels as well as in his plays. In all of us a *Tekla*, an *Adolph*, a *Gustav*—or a *Jean* and a *Miss Julia*—lie more or less dormant. And if we search our souls unsparingly, I fear the result can only be an admission that—had the needed set of circumstances been provided—we might have come unpleasantly close to one of those Strindbergian creatures which we are now inclined to reject as unhuman.

Here we have the secret of what I believe to be the great Swedish dramatist's strongest hold on our interest. How could it otherwise happen that so many critics, of such widely differing temperaments, have recorded identical feelings as springing from a study of his work: on one side an active resentment, a keen unwillingness to be interested; on the other, an attraction that would not be denied in spite of resolute resistance to it! For Strindberg *does* hold us, even when we regret his power of doing so. And no one familiar with the conclusions of modern psychology could imagine such a paradox possible did not the object of our sorely divided feelings provide us with something that our minds instinctively recognise as true to life in some way, and for that reason valuable to the art of living.

There are so many ways of presenting truth. Strindberg's is only one of them—and not the one commonly employed nowadays. Its main fault lies perhaps in being too intellectual, too abstract. For while Strindberg was intensely emotional, and while this fact colours all his writings, he could only express himself through his reason. An emotion that would move another man to murder would precipitate Strindberg into merciless analysis of his own or somebody else's mental and moral make-up. At any rate, I do not proclaim his way of presenting truth as the best one of all available. But I suspect that this decidedly strange way of Strindberg's—resulting in such repulsively superior beings as *Gustav*, or in such grievously inferior ones as *Adolph*—may come nearer the temper and needs of the future than do the ways of much more plausible writers. This does not need to imply that the future will imitate Strindberg. But it may ascertain what he aimed at doing, and then do it with a degree of perfection which he, the pioneer, could never hope to attain.

CREDITORS
A TRAGICOMEDY
1889

PERSONS

TEKLA
ADOLPH, her husband, a painter
GUSTAV, her divorced husband, a high-school teacher (who is travelling under an assumed name)

SCENE
(A parlor in a summer hotel on the sea-shore. The rear wall has a door opening on a veranda, beyond which is seen a landscape. To the right of the door stands a table with newspapers on it. There is a chair on the left side of the stage. To the right of the table stands a sofa. A door on the right leads to an adjoining room.)

(ADOLPH and GUSTAV, the latter seated on the sofa by the table to the right.)

ADOLPH. [At work on a wax figure on a miniature modelling stand; his crutches are placed beside him]—and for all this I have to thank you!

GUSTAV. [Smoking a cigar] Oh, nonsense!

ADOLPH. Why, certainly! During the first days after my wife had gone, I lay helpless on a sofa and did nothing but long for her. It was as if she had taken away my crutches with her, so that I couldn't move from the spot. When I had slept a couple of days, I seemed to come to, and began to pull myself together. My head calmed down after having been working feverishly. Old thoughts from days gone by bobbed up again. The desire to work and the instinct for creation came back. My eyes recovered their faculty of quick and straight vision—and then you showed up.

GUSTAV. I admit you were in a miserable condition when I first met you, and you had to use your crutches when you walked, but this is not to say that my presence has been the cause of your recovery. You needed a rest, and you had a craving for masculine company.

ADOLPH. Oh, that's true enough, like everything you say. Once I used to have men for friends, but I thought them superfluous after I married, and I felt quite satisfied with the one I had chosen. Later I was drawn into new circles and made a lot of acquaintances, but my wife was jealous of them—she wanted to keep me to herself: worse still—she wanted also to keep my friends to herself. And so I was left alone with my own jealousy.

GUSTAV. Yes, you have a strong tendency toward that kind of disease.

ADOLPH. I was afraid of losing her—and I tried to prevent it. There is nothing strange in that. But I was never afraid that she might be deceiving me—

GUSTAV. No, that's what married men are never afraid of.

ADOLPH. Yes, isn't it queer? What I really feared was that her friends would get such an influence over her that they would begin to exercise some kind of indirect power over me—and *that* is something I couldn't bear.

GUSTAV. So your ideas don't agree—yours and your wife's?

ADOLPH. Seeing that you have heard so much already, I may as well tell you everything. My wife has an independent nature—what are you smiling at?

GUSTAV. Go on! She has an independent nature—

ADOLPH. Which cannot accept anything from me—

GUSTAV. But from everybody else.

ADOLPH. [After a pause] Yes.—And it looked as if she especially hated my ideas because they were mine, and not because there was anything wrong about them. For it used to happen quite often that she advanced ideas that had once been mine, and that she stood up for them as her own. Yes, it even happened that friends of mine gave her ideas which they had taken directly from me, and then they seemed all right. Everything was all right except what came from me.

GUSTAV. Which means that you are not entirely happy?

ADOLPH. Oh yes, I am happy. I have the one I wanted, and I have never wanted anybody else.

GUSTAV. And you have never wanted to be free?

ADOLPH. No, I can't say that I have. Oh, well, sometimes I have imagined that it might seem like a rest to be free. But the moment she leaves me, I begin to long for her—long for her as for my own arms and legs. It is queer that sometimes I have a feeling that she is nothing in herself, but only a part of myself—an organ that can take away with it my will, my very desire to live. It seems almost as if I had deposited with her that centre of vitality of which the anatomical books tell us.

GUSTAV. Perhaps, when we get to the bottom of it, that is just what has happened.

ADOLPH. How could it be so? Is she not an independent being, with thoughts of her own? And when I met her I was nothing—a child of an artist whom she undertook to educate.

GUSTAV. But later you developed her thoughts and educated her, didn't you?

ADOLPH. No, she stopped growing and I pushed on.

GUSTAV. Yes, isn't it strange that her "authoring" seemed to fall off after her first book—or that it failed to improve, at least? But that first time she had a subject which wrote itself—for I understand she used her former husband for a model. You never knew him, did you? They say he was an idiot.

ADOLPH. I never knew him, as he was away for six months at a time. But he must have been an arch-idiot, judging by her picture of him. [Pause] And you may feel sure that the picture was correct.

GUSTAV. I do!—But why did she ever take him?

ADOLPH. Because she didn't know him well enough. Of course, you never *do* get acquainted until afterward!

GUSTAV. And for that reason one ought not to marry until— afterward.— And he was a tyrant, of course?

ADOLPH. Of course?

GUSTAV. Why, so are all married men. [Feeling his way] And you not the least.

ADOLPH. I? Who let my wife come and go as she pleases—

GUSTAV. Well, that's nothing. You couldn't lock her up, could you? But do you like her to stay away whole nights?

ADOLPH. No, really, I don't.

GUSTAV. There, you see! [With a change of tactics] And to tell the truth, it would only make you ridiculous to like it.

ADOLPH. Ridiculous? Can a man be ridiculous because he trusts his wife?

GUSTAV. Of course he can. And it's just what you are already—and thoroughly at that!

ADOLPH. [Convulsively] I! It's what I dread most of all—and there's going to be a change.

GUSTAV. Don't get excited now—or you'll have another attack.

ADOLPH. But why isn't she ridiculous when I stay out all night?

GUSTAV. Yes, why? Well, it's nothing that concerns you, but that's the way it is. And while you are trying to figure out why, the mishap has already occurred.

ADOLPH. What mishap?

GUSTAV. However, the first husband was a tyrant, and she took him only to get her freedom. You see, a girl cannot have freedom except by providing herself with a chaperon—or what we call a husband.

ADOLPH. Of course not.

GUSTAV. And now you are the chaperon.

ADOLPH. I?

GUSTAV. Since you are her husband.

(ADOLPH keeps a preoccupied silence.)

GUSTAV. Am I not right?

ADOLPH. [Uneasily] I don't know. You live with a woman for years, and you never stop to analyse her, or your relationship with her, and then—then you begin to think—and there you are!—Gustav, you are my friend. The only male friend I have. During this last week you have given me courage to live again. It is as if your own magnetism had been poured into me. Like a watchmaker, you have fixed the works in my head and wound up the spring again. Can't you hear, yourself, how I think more clearly and speak more to the point? And to myself at least it seems as if my voice had recovered its ring.

GUSTAV. So it seems to me also. And why is that?

ADOLPH. I shouldn't wonder if you grew accustomed to lower your voice in talking to women. I know at least that Tekla always used to accuse me of shouting.

GUSTAV. And so you toned down your voice and accepted the rule of the slipper?

ADOLPH. That isn't quite the way to put it. [After some reflection] I think it is even worse than that. But let us talk of something else!—What was I saying?—Yes, you came here, and you enabled me to see my art in its true light. Of course, for some time I had noticed my growing lack of interest in painting, as it didn't seem to offer me the proper medium for the expression of what I wanted to bring out. But when you explained all this to me, and made it clear why painting must fail as a timely outlet for the creative instinct, then I saw the light at last—and I realised that hereafter it would not be possible for me to express myself by means of colour only.

GUSTAV. Are you quite sure now that you cannot go on painting— that you may not have a relapse?

ADOLPH. Perfectly sure! For I have tested myself. When I went to bed that night after our talk, I rehearsed your argument point by point, and I knew you had it right. But when I woke up from a good night's sleep and my head was clear again, then it came over me in a flash that you might be mistaken after all. And I jumped out of bed and got hold of my brushes and paints—but it was no use! Every trace of illusion was gone—it was nothing but smears of paint, and I quaked at the thought of having believed, and having made others believe, that a painted canvas could be anything but a painted canvas. The veil had fallen from my eyes, and it was just as impossible for me to paint any more as it was to become a child again.

GUSTAV. And then you saw that the realistic tendency of our day, its craving for actuality and tangibility, could only find its proper form in sculpture, which gives you body, extension in all three dimensions—

ADOLPH. [Vaguely] The three dimensions—oh yes, body, in a word!

GUSTAV. And then you became a sculptor yourself. Or rather, you have been one all your life, but you had gone astray, and nothing was needed but a guide to put you on the right road—Tell me, do you experience supreme joy now when you are at work?

ADOLPH. Now I am living!

GUSTAV. May I see what you are doing?

ADOLPH. A female figure.

GUSTAV. Without a model? And so lifelike at that!

ADOLPH. [Apathetically] Yes, but it resembles somebody. It is remarkable that this woman seems to have become a part of my body as I of hers.

GUSTAV. Well, that's not so very remarkable. Do you know what transfusion is?

ADOLPH. Of blood? Yes.

GUSTAV. And you seem to have bled yourself a little too much. When I look at the figure here I comprehend several things which I merely guessed before. You have loved her tremendously!

ADOLPH. Yes, to such an extent that I couldn't tell whether she was I or I she. When she is smiling, I smile also. When she is weeping, I weep. And when she—can you imagine anything like it?— when she was giving life to our child— I felt the birth pangs within myself.

GUSTAV. Do you know, my dear friend—I hate to speak of it, but you are already showing the first symptoms of epilepsy.

ADOLPH. [Agitated] I! How can you tell?

GUSTAV. Because I have watched the symptoms in a younger brother of mine who had been worshipping Venus a little too excessively.

ADOLPH. How—how did it show itself—that thing you spoke of?

[During the following passage GUSTAV speaks with great animation, and ADOLPH listens so intently that, unconsciously, he imitates many of GUSTAV'S gestures.]

GUSTAV. It was dreadful to witness, and if you don't feel strong enough I won't inflict a description of it on you.

ADOLPH. [Nervously] Yes, go right on—just go on!

GUSTAV. Well, the boy happened to marry an innocent little creature with curls, and eyes like a turtle-dove; with the face of a child and the pure soul of an angel. But nevertheless she managed to usurp the male prerogative—

ADOLPH. What is that?

GUSTAV. Initiative, of course. And with the result that the angel nearly carried him off to heaven. But first he had to be put on the cross and made to feel the nails in his flesh. It was horrible!

ADOLPH. [Breathlessly] Well, what happened?

GUSTAV. [Lingering on each word] We might be sitting together talking, he and I—and when I had been speaking for a while his face would turn white as chalk, his arms and legs would grow stiff, and his thumbs became twisted against the palms of his hands—like this. [He illustrates the movement and it is imitated by ADOLPH] Then his eyes became bloodshot, and he began to chew— like this. [He chews, and again ADOLPH imitates him] The saliva was rattling in his throat. His chest was squeezed together as if it had been closed in a vice. The pupils of his eyes flickered like gas-jets. His tongue beat the saliva into a lather, and he sank—slowly—down—backward—into the chair—as if he were drowning. And then—

ADOLPH. [In a whisper] Stop now!

GUSTAV. And then—Are you not feeling well?

ADOLPH. No.

GUSTAV. [Gets a glass of water for him] There: drink now. And we'll talk of something else.

ADOLPH. [Feebly] Thank you! Please go on!

GUSTAV. Well—when he came to he couldn't remember anything at all. He had simply lost consciousness. Has that ever happened to you?

ADOLPH. Yes, I have had attacks of vertigo now and then, but my physician says it's only anaemia.

GUSTAV. Well, that's the beginning of it, you know. But, believe me, it will end in epilepsy if you don't take care of yourself.

ADOLPH. What can I do?

GUSTAV. To begin with, you will have to observe complete abstinence.

ADOLPH. For how long?

GUSTAV. For half a year at least.

ADOLPH. I cannot do it. That would upset our married life.

GUSTAV. Good-bye to you then!

ADOLPH. [Covers up the wax figure] I cannot do it!

GUSTAV. Can you not save your own life?—But tell me, as you have already given me so much of your confidence—is there no other canker, no secret wound, that troubles you? For it is very rare to find only one cause of discord, as life is so full of variety and so fruitful in chances for false relationships. Is there not a corpse in your cargo that you are trying to hide from yourself?— For instance, you said a minute ago that you have a child which has been left in other people's care. Why don't you keep it with you?

ADOLPH. My wife doesn't want us to do so.

GUSTAV. And her reason? Speak up now!

ADOLPH. Because, when it was about three years old, it began to look like him, her former husband.

GUSTAV. Well? Have you seen her former husband?

ADOLPH. No, never. I have only had a casual glance at a very poor portrait of him, and then I couldn't detect the slightest resemblance.

GUSTAV. Oh, portraits are never like the original, and, besides, he might have changed considerably since it was made. However, I hope it hasn't aroused any suspicions in you?

ADOLPH. Not at all. The child was born a year after our marriage, and the husband was abroad when I first met Tekla—it happened right here, in this very house even, and that's why we come here every summer.

GUSTAV. No, then there can be no cause for suspicion. And you wouldn't have had any reason to trouble yourself anyhow, for the children of a widow who marries again often show a likeness to her dead husband. It is annoying, of course, and that's why they used to burn all widows in India, as you know.—But tell me: have you ever felt jealous of him—of his memory? Would it not sicken you to meet him on a walk and hear him, with his eyes on your Tekla, use the word "we" instead of "I"?—We!

ADOLPH. I cannot deny that I have been pursued by that very thought.

GUSTAV. There now!—And you'll never get rid of it. There are discords in this life which can never be reduced to harmony. For this reason you had better put wax in your ears and go to work. If you work, and grow old, and pile masses of new impressions on the hatches, then the corpse will stay quiet in the hold.

ADOLPH. Pardon me for interrupting you, but—it is wonderful how you resemble Tekla now and then while you are talking. You have a way of blinking one eye as if you were taking aim with a gun, and your eyes have the same influence on me as hers have at times.

GUSTAV. No, really?

ADOLPH. And now you said that "no, really" in the same indifferent way that she does. She also has the habit of saying "no, really" quite often.

GUSTAV. Perhaps we are distantly related, seeing that all human beings are said to be of one family. At any rate, it will be interesting to make your wife's acquaintance to see if what you say is true.

ADOLPH. And do you know, she never takes an expression from me. She seems rather to avoid my vocabulary, and I have never caught her using any of my gestures. And yet people as a rule develop what is called "marital resemblance."

GUSTAV. And do you know why this has not happened in your case?—That woman has never loved you.

ADOLPH. What do you mean?

GUSTAV. I hope you will excuse what I am saying—but woman's love consists in taking, in receiving, and one from whom she takes nothing does not have her love. She has never loved you!

ADOLPH. Don't you think her capable of loving more than once?

GUSTAV. No, for we cannot be deceived more than once. Then our eyes are opened once for all. You have never been deceived, and so you had better beware of those that have. They are dangerous, I tell you.

ADOLPH. Your words pierce me like knife thrusts, and I fool as if something were being severed within me, but I cannot help it. And this cutting brings a certain relief, too. For it means the pricking of ulcers that never seemed to ripen.—She has never loved me!—Why, then, did she ever take me?

GUSTAV. Tell me first how she came to take you, and whether it was you who took her or she who took you?

ADOLPH. Heaven only knows if I can tell at all!—How did it happen? Well, it didn't come about in one day.

GUSTAV. Would you like to have me tell you how it did happen?

ADOLPH. That's more than you can do.

GUSTAV. Oh, by using the information about yourself and your wife that you have given me, I think I can reconstruct the whole event. Listen now, and you'll hear. [In a dispassionate tone, almost humorously] The husband had gone abroad to study, and she was alone. At first her freedom seemed rather pleasant. Then came a sense of vacancy, for I presume she was pretty empty when she had lived by herself for a fortnight. Then *he* appeared, and by and by the vacancy was filled up. By comparison the absent one seemed to fade out, and for the simple reason that he was at a distance—you know the law about the square of the distance? But when they felt their passions stirring, then came fear—of themselves, of their consciences, of him. For protection they played brother and sister. And the more their feelings smacked of the flesh, the more they tried to make their relationship appear spiritual.

ADOLPH. Brother and sister? How could you know that?

GUSTAV. I guessed it. Children are in the habit of playing papa and mamma, but when they grow up they play brother and sister—in order to hide what should be hidden!—And then they took the vow of chastity—and then they played hide-and-seek—until they got in a dark corner where they were sure of not being seen by anybody. [With mock severity] But they felt that there was *one* whose eye reached them in the darkness—and they grew frightened— and their fright raised the spectre of the absent one—his figure began to assume immense proportions—it became metamorphosed: turned into a nightmare that disturbed their amorous slumbers; a creditor who knocked at all doors. Then they saw his black hand between their own as these sneaked toward each other across the table; and they heard his grating voice through that stillness of the night that should have been broken only by the beating of their own pulses. He did not prevent them from possessing each other but he spoiled their happiness. And when they became aware of his invisible interference with their happiness; when they took flight at last—a vain flight from the memories that pursued them, from the liability they had left behind, from the public opinion they could not face—and when they found themselves without the strength needed to carry their own guilt, then they had to send out into the fields for a scapegoat to be sacrificed. They were free-thinkers, but they did not have the courage to step forward and speak openly to him the words: "We love each other!" To sum it up, they were cowards, and so the tyrant had to be slaughtered. Is that right?

ADOLPH. Yes, but you forget that she educated me, that she filled my head with new thoughts—

GUSTAV. I have not forgotten it. But tell me: why could she not educate the other man also—into a free-thinker?

ADOLPH. Oh, he was an idiot!

GUSTAV. Oh, of course—he was an idiot! But that's rather an ambiguous term, and, as pictured in her novel, his idiocy seems mainly to have consisted in failure to understand her. Pardon me a question: but is your wife so very profound after all? I have discovered nothing profound in her writings.

ADOLPH. Neither have I.—But then I have also to confess a certain difficulty in understanding her. It is as if the cogs of our brain wheels didn't fit into each other, and as if something went to pieces in my head when I try to comprehend her.

GUSTAV. Maybe you are an idiot, too?

ADOLPH. I don't *think* so! And it seems to me all the time as if she were in the wrong—Would you care to read this letter, for instance, which I got today?

[Takes out a letter from his pocket-book.]

GUSTAV. [Glancing through the letter] Hm! The handwriting seems strangely familiar.

ADOLPH. Rather masculine, don't you think?

GUSTAV. Well, I know at least *one* man who writes that kind of hand—She addresses you as "brother." Are you still playing comedy to each other? And do you never permit yourselves any greater familiarity in speaking to each other?

ADOLPH. No, it seems to me that all mutual respect is lost in that way.

GUSTAV. And is it to make you respect her that she calls herself your sister?

ADOLPH. I want to respect her more than myself. I want her to be the better part of my own self.

GUSTAV. Why don't you be that better part yourself? Would it be less convenient than to permit somebody else to fill the part? Do you want to place yourself beneath your wife?

ADOLPH. Yes, I do. I take a pleasure in never quite reaching up to her. I have taught her to swim, for example, and now I enjoy hearing her boast that she surpasses me both in skill and daring. To begin with, I merely pretended to be awkward and timid in order to raise her courage. And so it ended with my actually being her inferior, more of a coward than she. It almost seemed to me as if she had actually taken my courage away from me.

GUSTAV. Have you taught her anything else?

ADOLPH. Yes—but it must stay between us—I have taught her how to spell, which she didn't know before. But now, listen: when she took charge of our domestic correspondence, I grew out of the habit of writing. And think of it: as the years passed on, lack of practice made me forget a little here and there of my grammar. But do you think she recalls that I was the one who taught her at the start? No—and so I am "the idiot," of course.

GUSTAV. So you *are* an idiot already?

ADOLPH. Oh, it's just a joke, of course!

GUSTAV. Of course! But this is clear cannibalism, I think. Do you know what's behind that sort of practice? The savages eat their enemies in order to acquire their useful qualities. And this woman has been eating your soul, your courage, your knowledge—

ADOLPH. And my faith! It was I who urged her to write her first book—

GUSTAV. [Making a face] Oh-h-h!

ADOLPH. It was I who praised her, even when I found her stuff rather poor. It was I who brought her into literary circles where she could gather honey from our most ornamental literary flowers. It was I who used my personal influence to keep the critics from her throat. It was I who blew her faith in herself into flame; blew on it until I lost my own breath. I gave, gave, gave— until I had nothing left for myself. Do you know—I'll tell you everything now— do you know I really believe—and the human soul is so peculiarly constituted— I believe that when my artistic successes seemed about to put her in the shadow—as well as her reputation— then I tried to put courage into her by belittling myself, and by making my own art seem inferior to hers. I talked so long about the insignificant part played by painting on the whole—talked so long about it, and invented so many reasons to prove what I said, that one fine day I found myself convinced of its futility. So all you had to do was to breathe on a house of cards.

GUSTAV. Pardon me for recalling what you said at the beginning of our talk—that she had never taken anything from you.

ADOLPH. She doesn't nowadays. Because there is nothing more to take.

GUSTAV. The snake being full, it vomits now.

ADOLPH. Perhaps she has been taking a good deal more from me than I have been aware of?

GUSTAV. You can be sure of that. She took when you were not looking, and that is called theft.

ADOLPH. Perhaps she never did educate me?

GUSTAV. But you her? In all likelihood! But it was her trick to make it appear the other way to you. May I ask how she set about educating you?

ADOLPH. Oh, first of all—hm!

GUSTAV. Well?

ADOLPH. Well, I—

GUSTAV. No, we were speaking of her.

ADOLPH. Really, I cannot tell now.

GUSTAV. Do you see!

ADOLPH. However—she devoured my faith also, and so I sank further and further down, until you came along and gave me a new faith.

GUSTAV. [Smiling] In sculpture?

ADOLPH. [Doubtfully] Yes.

GUSTAV. And have you really faith in it? In this abstract, antiquated art that dates back to the childhood of civilisation? Do you believe that you can obtain your effect by pure form—by the three dimensions—tell me? That you can reach the practical mind of our own day, and convey an illusion to it, without the use of colour—without colour, mind you—do you really believe that?

ADOLPH. [Crushed] No!

GUSTAV. Well, I don't either.

ADOLPH. Why, then, did you say you did?

GUSTAV. Because I pitied you.

ADOLPH. Yes, I am to be pitied! For now I am bankrupt! Finished!— And worst of all: not even she is left to me!

GUSTAV. Well, what could you do with her?

ADOLPH. Oh, she would be to me what God was before I became an atheist: an object that might help me to exercise my sense of veneration.

GUSTAV. Bury your sense of veneration and let something else grow on top of it. A little wholesome scorn, for instance.

ADOLPH. I cannot live without having something to respect—

GUSTAV. Slave!

ADOLPH.—without a woman to respect and worship!

GUSTAV. Oh, HELL! Then you had better take back your God—if you needs must have something to kow-tow to! You're a fine atheist, with all that superstition about woman still in you! You're a fine free-thinker, who dare not think freely about the dear ladies! Do you know what that incomprehensible, sphinx-like, profound something in your wife really is? It is sheer stupidity!—Look here: she cannot even distinguish between th and t. And that, you know, means there is something wrong with the mechanism. When you look at the case, it looks like a chronometer, but the works inside are those of an ordinary cheap watch.—Nothing but the skirts-that's all! Put trousers on her, give her a pair of moustaches of soot under her nose, then take a good, sober look at her, and listen to her in the same manner: you'll find the instrument has another sound to it. A phonograph, and nothing else—giving you back your own words, or those of other people—and always in diluted form. Have you ever looked at a naked woman— oh yes, yes, of course! A youth with over-developed breasts; an under-developed man; a child that has shot up to full height and then stopped growing in other respects; one who is chronically anaemic: what can you expect of such a creature?

ADOLPH. Supposing all that to be true—how can it be possible that I still think her my equal?

GUSTAV. Hallucination—the hypnotising power of skirts! Or—the two of you may actually have become equals. The levelling process has been finished. Her capillarity has brought the water in both tubes to the same height.—Tell me [taking out his watch]: our talk has now lasted six hours, and your wife ought soon to be here. Don't you think we had better stop, so that you can get a rest?

ADOLPH. No, don't leave me! I don't dare to be alone!

GUSTAV. Oh, for a little while only—and then the lady will come.

ADOLPH. Yes, she is coming!—It's all so queer! I long for her, but I am afraid of her. She pets me, she is tender to me, but there is suffocation in her kisses—something that pulls and numbs. And I feel like a circus child that is being pinched by the clown in order that it may look rosy-cheeked when it appears before the public.

GUSTAV. I feel very sorry for you, my friend. Without being a physician, I can tell that you are a dying man. It is enough to look at your latest pictures in order to see that.

ADOLPH. You think so? How can you see it?

GUSTAV. Your colour is watery blue, anaemic, thin, so that the cadaverous yellow of the canvas shines through. And it impresses me as if your own hollow, putty-coloured checks were showing beneath—

ADOLPH. Oh, stop, stop!

GUSTAV. Well, this is not only my personal opinion. Have you read to-day's paper?

ADOLPH. [Shrinking] No!

GUSTAV. It's on the table here.

ADOLPH. [Reaching for the paper without daring to take hold of it] Do they speak of it there?

GUSTAV. Read it—or do you want me to read it to you?

ADOLPH. No!

GUSTAV. I'll leave you, if you want me to.

ADOLPH. No, no, no!—I don't know—it seems as if I were beginning to hate you, and yet I cannot let you go.—You drag me out of the hole into which I have fallen, but no sooner do you get me on firm ice, than you knock me on the head and shove me into the water again. As long as my secrets were my own, I had still something left within me, but now I am quite empty. There is a canvas by an Italian master, showing a scene of torture—a saint whose intestines are being torn out of him and rolled on the axle of a windlass. The martyr is watching himself grow thinner and thinner, while the roll on the axle grows thicker.—Now it seems to me as if you had swelled out since you began to dig in me; and when you leave, you'll carry away my vitals with you, and leave nothing but an empty shell behind.

GUSTAV. How you do let your fancy run away with you!—And besides, your wife is bringing back your heart.

ADOLPH. No, not since you have burned her to ashes. Everything is in ashes where you have passed along: my art, my love, my hope, my faith!

GUSTAV. All of it was pretty nearly finished before I came along.

ADOLPH. Yes, but it might have been saved. Now it's too late—incendiary!

GUSTAV. We have cleared some ground only. Now we'll sow in the ashes.

ADOLPH. I hate you! I curse you!

GUSTAV. Good symptoms! There is still some strength left in you. And now I'll pull you up on the ice again. Listen now! Do you want to listen to me, and do you want to obey me?

ADOLPH. Do with me what you will—I'll obey you!

GUSTAV. [Rising] Look at me!

ADOLPH. [Looking at GUSTAV] Now you are looking at me again with that other pair of eyes which attracts me.

GUSTAV. And listen to me!

ADOLPH. Yes, but speak of yourself. Don't talk of me any longer: I am like an open wound and cannot bear being touched.

GUSTAV. No, there is nothing to say about me. I am a teacher of dead languages, and a widower—that's all! Take my hand.

ADOLPH. What terrible power there must be in you! It feels as if I were touching an electrical generator.

GUSTAV. And bear in mind that I have been as weak as you are now.—Stand up!

ADOLPH. [Rises, but keeps himself from falling only by throwing his arms around the neck of GUSTAV] I am like a boneless baby, and my brain seems to lie bare.

GUSTAV. Take a turn across the floor!

ADOLPH. I cannot!

GUSTAV. Do what I say, or I'll strike you!

ADOLPH. [Straightening himself up] What are you saying?

GUSTAV. I'll strike you, I said.

ADOLPH. [Leaping backward in a rage] You!

GUSTAV. That's it! Now you have got the blood into your head, and your self-assurance is awake. And now I'll give you some electriticy: where is your wife?

ADOLPH. Where is she?

GUSTAV. Yes.

ADOLPH. She is—at—a meeting.

GUSTAV. Sure?

ADOLPH. Absolutely!

GUSTAV. What kind of meeting?

ADOLPH. Oh, something relating to an orphan asylum.

GUSTAV. Did you part as friends?

ADOLPH. [With some hesitation] Not as friends.

GUSTAV. As enemies then!—What did you say that provoked her?

ADOLPH. You are terrible. I am afraid of you. How could you know?

GUSTAV. It's very simple: I possess three known factors, and with their help I figure out the unknown one. What did you say to her?

ADOLPH. I said—two words only, but they were dreadful, and I regret them—regret them very much.

GUSTAV. Don't do it! Tell me now?

ADOLPH. I said: "Old flirt!"

GUSTAV. What more did you say?

ADOLPH. Nothing at all.

GUSTAV. Yes, you did, but you have forgotten it—perhaps because you don't dare remember it. You have put it away in a secret drawer, but you have got to open it now!

ADOLPH. I can't remember!

GUSTAV. But I know. This is what you said: "You ought to be ashamed of flirting when you are too old to have any more lovers!"

ADOLPH. Did I say that? I must have said it!—But how can you know that I did?

GUSTAV. I heard her tell the story on board the boat as I came here.

ADOLPH. To whom?

GUSTAV. To four young men who formed her company. She is already developing a taste for chaste young men, just like—

ADOLPH. But there is nothing wrong in that?

GUSTAV. No more than in playing brother and sister when you are papa and mamma.

ADOLPH. So you have seen her then?

GUSTAV. Yes, I have. But you have never seen her when you didn't— I mean, when you were not present. And there's the reason, you see, why a husband can never really know his wife. Have you a portrait of her?

(Adolph takes a photograph from his pocketbook. There is a look of aroused curiosity on his face.)

GUSTAV. You were not present when this was taken?

ADOLPH. No.

GUSTAV. Look at it. Does it bear much resemblance to the portrait you painted of her? Hardly any! The features are the same, but the expression is quite different. But you don't see this, because your own picture of her creeps in between your eyes and this one. Look at it now as a painter, without giving a thought to the original. What does it represent? Nothing, so far as I can see, but an affected coquette inviting somebody to come and play with her. Do you notice this cynical line around the mouth which you are never allowed to see? Can you see that her eyes are seeking out some man who is not you? Do you observe that her dress is cut low at the neck, that her hair is done up in a different way, that her sleeve has managed to slip back from her arm? Can you see?

ADOLPH. Yes—now I see.

GUSTAV. Look out, my boy!

ADOLPH. For what?

GUSTAV. For her revenge! Bear in mind that when you said she could not attract a man, you struck at what to her is most sacred—the one thing above all others. If you had told her that she wrote nothing but nonsense, she would have laughed at your poor taste. But as it is—believe me, it will not be her fault if her desire for revenge has not already been satisfied.

ADOLPH. I must know if it is so!

GUSTAV. Find out!

ADOLPH. Find out?

GUSTAV. Watch—I'll assist you, if you want me to.

ADOLPH. As I am to die anyhow—it may as well come first as last! What am I to do?

GUSTAV. First of all a piece of information: has your wife any vulnerable point?

ADOLPH. Hardly! I think she must have nine lives, like a cat.

GUSTAV. There—that was the boat whistling at the landing—now she'll soon be here.

ADOLPH. Then I must go down and meet her.

GUSTAV. No, you are to stay here. You have to be impolite. If her conscience is clear, you'll catch it until your ears tingle. If she is guilty, she'll come up and pet you.

ADOLPH. Are you so sure of that?

GUSTAV. Not quite, because a rabbit will sometimes turn and run in loops, but I'll follow. My room is nest to this. [He points to the door on the right] There I shall take up my position and watch you while you are playing the game in here. But when you are done, we'll change parts: I'll enter the cage and do tricks with the snake while you stick to the key-hole. Then we meet in the park to compare notes. But keep your back stiff. And if you feel yourself weakening, knock twice on the floor with a chair.

ADOLPH. All right!—But don't go away. I must be sure that you are in the next room.

GUSTAV. You can be quite sure of that. But don't get scared afterward, when you watch me dissecting a human soul and laying out its various parts on the table. They say it is rather hard on a beginner, but once you have seen it done, you never want to miss it.—And be sure to remember one thing: not a word about having met me, or having made any new acquaintance whatever while she was away. Not one word! And I'll discover her weak point by myself. Hush, she has arrived—she is in her room now. She's humming to herself. That means she is in a rage!—Now, straight in the back, please! And sit down on that chair over there, so that she has to sit here—then I can watch both of you at the same time.

ADOLPH. It's only fifteen minutes to dinner—and no new guests have arrived—for I haven't heard the bell ring. That means we shall be by ourselves—worse luck!

GUSTAV. Are you weak?

ADOLPH. I am nothing at all!—Yes, I am afraid of what is now coming!

But I cannot keep it from coming! The stone has been set rolling—and it was not the first drop of water that started it— nor wad it the last one—but all of them together.

GUSTAV. Let it roll then—for peace will come in no other way. Good-bye for a while now! [Goes out]

(ADOLPH nods back at him. Until then he has been standing with the photograph in his hand. Now he tears it up and flings the pieces under the table. Then he sits down on a chair, pulls nervously at his tie, runs his fingers through his hair, crumples his coat lapel, and so on.)

TEKLA. [Enters, goes straight up to him and gives him a kiss; her manner is friendly, frank, happy, and engaging] Hello, little brother! How is he getting on?

ADOLPH. [Almost won over; speaking reluctantly and as if in jest] What mischief have you been up to now that makes you come and kiss me?

TEKLA. I'll tell you: I've spent an awful lot of money.

ADOLPH. You have had a good time then?

TEKLA. Very! But not exactly at that crèche meeting. That was plain piffle, to tell the truth.—But what has little brother found to divert himself with while his Pussy was away?

(Her eyes wander around the room as if she were looking for somebody or sniffing something.)

ADOLPH. I've simply been bored.

TEKLA. And no company at all?

ADOLPH. Quite by myself.

TEKLA. [Watching him; she sits down on the sofa] Who has been sitting here? ADOLPH. Over there? Nobody.

TEKLA. That's funny! The seat is still warm, and there is a hollow here that looks as if it had been made by an elbow. Have you had lady callers?

ADOLPH. I? You don't believe it, do you?

TEKLA. But you blush. I think little brother is not telling the truth. Come and tell Pussy now what he has on his conscience.

(Draws him toward herself so that he sinks down with his head resting in her lap.)

ADOLPH. You're a little devil—do you know that?

TEKLA. No, I don't know anything at all about myself.

ADOLPH. You never think about yourself, do you?

TEKLA. [Sniffing and taking notes] I think of nothing but myself— I am a dreadful egoist. But what has made you turn so philosophical all at once?

ADOLPH. Put your hand on my forehead.

TEKLA. [Prattling as if to a baby] Has he got ants in his head again? Does he want me to take them away, does he? [Kisses him on the forehead] There now! Is it all right now?

ADOLPH. Now it's all right. [Pause]

TEKLA. Well, tell me now what you have been doing to make the time go? Have you painted anything?

ADOLPH. No, I am done with painting.

TEKLA. What? Done with painting?

ADOLPH. Yes, but don't scold me for it. How can I help it that I can't paint any longer!

TEKLA. What do you mean to do then?

ADOLPH. I'll become a sculptor.

TEKLA. What a lot of brand new ideas again!

ADOLPH. Yes, but please don't scold! Look at that figure over there.

TEKLA. [Uncovering the wax figure] Well, I declare!—Who is that meant for?

ADOLPH. Guess!

TEKLA. Is it Pussy? Has he got no shame at all?

ADOLPH. Is it like?

TEKLA. How can I tell when there is no face?

ADOLPH. Yes, but there is so much else—that's beautiful!

TEKLA. [Taps him playfully on the cheek] Now he must keep still or I'll have to kiss him.

ADOLPH. [Holding her back] Now, now!—Somebody might come!

TEKLA. Well, what do I care? Can't I kiss my own husband, perhaps? Oh yes, that's my lawful right.

ADOLPH. Yes, but don't you know—in the hotel here, they don't believe we are married, because we are kissing each other such a lot. And it makes no difference that we quarrel now and then, for lovers are said to do that also.

TEKLA. Well, but what's the use of quarrelling? Why can't he always be as nice as he is now? Tell me now? Can't he try? Doesn't he want us to be happy?

ADOLPH. Do I want it? Yes, but—

TEKLA. There we are again! Who has put it into his head that he is not to paint any longer?

ADOLPH. Who? You are always looking for somebody else behind me and my thoughts. Are you jealous?

TEKLA. Yes, I am. I'm afraid somebody might take him away from me.

ADOLPH. Are you really afraid of that? You who know that no other woman can take your place, and that I cannot live without you!

TEKLA. Well, I am not afraid of the women—it's your friends that fill your head with all sorts of notions.

ADOLPH. [Watching her] You are afraid then? Of what are you afraid?

TEKLA. [Getting up] Somebody has been here. Who has been here?

ADOLPH. Don't you wish me to look at you?

TEKLA. Not in that way: it's not the way you are accustomed to look at me.

ADOLPH. How was I looking at you then?

TEKLA. Way up under my eyelids.

ADOLPH. Under your eyelids—yes, I wanted to see what is behind them.

TEKLA. See all you can! There is nothing that needs to be hidden. But—you talk differently, too—you use expressions—[studying him] you philosophise—that's what you do! [Approaches him threateningly] Who has been here?

ADOLPH. Nobody but my physician.

TEKLA. Your physician? Who is he?

ADOLPH. That doctor from Strömstad.

TEKLA. What's his name?

ADOLPH. Sjöberg.

TEKLA. What did he have to say?

ADOLPH. He said—well—among other things he said—that I am on the verge of epilepsy—

TEKLA. Among other things? What more did he say?

ADOLPH. Something very unpleasant.

TEKLA. Tell me!

ADOLPH. He forbade us to live as man and wife for a while.

TEKLA. Oh, that's it! Didn't I just guess it! They want to separate us! That's what I have understood a long time!

ADOLPH. You can't have understood, because there was nothing to understand.

TEKLA. Oh yes, I have!

ADOLPH. How can you see what doesn't exist, unless your fear of something has stirred up your fancy into seeing what has never existed? What is it you fear? That I might borrow somebody else's eyes in order to see you as you are, and not as you seem to be?

TEKLA. Keep your imagination in check, Adolph! It is the beast that dwells in man's soul.

ADOLPH. Where did you learn that? From those chaste young men on the boat—did you?

TEKLA. [Not at all abashed] Yes, there is something to be learned from youth also.

ADOLPH. I think you are already beginning to have a taste for youth?

TEKLA. I have always liked youth. That's why I love you. Do you object?

ADOLPH. No, but I should prefer to have no partners.

TEKLA. [Prattling roguishly] My heart is so big, little brother, that there is room in it for many more than him.

ADOLPH. But little brother doesn't want any more brothers.

TEKLA. Come here to Pussy now and get his hair pulled because he is jealous—no, envious is the right word for it!

(Two knocks with a chair are heard from the adjoining room, where GUSTAV is.)

ADOLPH. No, I don't want to play now. I want to talk seriously.

TEKLA. [Prattling] Mercy me, does he want to talk seriously? Dreadful, how serious he's become! [Takes hold of his head and kisses him] Smile a little—there now!

ADOLPH. [Smiling against his will] Oh, you're the—I might almost think you knew how to use magic!

TEKLA. Well, can't he see now? That's why he shouldn't start any trouble—or I might use my magic to make him invisible!

ADOLPH. [Gets up] Will you sit for me a moment, Tekla? With the side of your face this way, so that I can put a face on my figure.

TEKLA. Of course, I will.

[Turns her head so he can see her in profile.]

ADOLPH. [Gazes hard at her while pretending to work at the figure] Don't think of me now—but of somebody else.

TEKLA. I'll think of my latest conquest.

ADOLPH. That chaste young man?

TEKLA. Exactly! He had a pair of the prettiest, sweetest moustaches, and his cheek looked like a peach—it was so soft and rosy that you just wanted to bite it.

ADOLPH. [Darkening] Please keep that expression about the mouth.

TEKLA. What expression?

ADOLPH. A cynical, brazen one that I have never seen before.

TEKLA. [Making a face] This one?

ADOLPH. Just that one! [Getting up] Do you know how Bret Harte pictures an adulteress?

TEKLA. [Smiling] No, I have never read Bret Something.

ADOLPH. As a pale creature that cannot blush.

TEKLA. Not at all? But when she meets her lover, then she must blush, I am sure, although her husband or Mr. Bret may not be allowed to see it.

ADOLPH. Are you so sure of that?

TEKLA. [As before] Of course, as the husband is not capable of bringing the blood up to her head, he cannot hope to behold the charming spectacle.

ADOLPH. [Enraged] Tekla!

TEKLA. Oh, you little ninny!

ADOLPH. Tekla!

TEKLA. He should call her Pussy—then I might get up a pretty little blush for his sake. Does he want me to?

ADOLPH. [Disarmed] You minx, I'm so angry with you, that I could bite you!

TEKLA. [Playfully] Come and bite me then!—Come!

[Opens her arms to him.]

ADOLPH. [Puts his hands around her neck and kisses her] Yes, I'll bite you to death!

TEKLA. [Teasingly] Look out—somebody might come!

ADOLPH. Well, what do I care! I care for nothing else in the world if I can only have you!

TEKLA. And when, you don't have me any longer?

ADOLPH. Then I shall die!

TEKLA. But you are not afraid of losing me, are you—as I am too old to be wanted by anybody else?

ADOLPH. You have not forgotten my words yet, Tekla! I take it all back now!

TEKLA. Can you explain to me why you are at once so jealous and so cock-sure?

ADOLPH. No, I cannot explain anything at all. But it's possible that the thought of somebody else having possessed you may still be gnawing within me. At times it appears to me as if our love were nothing but a fiction, an attempt at self-defence, a passion kept up as a matter of honor—and I can't think of anything that would give me more pain than to have *him* know that I am unhappy. Oh, I have never seen him—but the mere thought that a person exists who is waiting for my misfortune to arrive, who is daily calling down curses on my head, who will roar with laughter when I perish—the mere idea of it obsesses me, drives me nearer to you, fascinates me, paralyses me!

TEKLA. Do you think I would let him have that joy? Do you think I would make his prophecy come true?

ADOLPH. No, I cannot think you would.

TEKLA. Why don't you keep calm then?

ADOLPH. No, you upset me constantly by your coquetry. Why do you play that kind of game?

TEKLA. It is no game. I want to be admired—that's all!

ADOLPH. Yes, but only by men!

TEKLA. Of course! For a woman is never admired by other women.

ADOLPH. Tell me, have you heard anything—from him—recently?

TEKLA. Not in the last sis months.

ADOLPH. Do you ever think of him?

TEKLA. No!—Since the child died we have broken off our correspondence.

ADOLPH. And you have never seen him at all?

TEKLA. No, I understand he is living somewhere down on the West Coast. But why is all this coming into your head just now?

ADOLPH. I don't know. But during the last few days, while I was alone, I kept thinking of him—how he might have felt when he was left alone that time.

TEKLA. Are you having an attack of bad conscience?

ADOLPH. I am.

TEKLA. You feel like a thief, do you?

ADOLPH. Almost!

TEKLA. Isn't that lovely! Women can be stolen as you steal children or chickens? And you regard me as his chattel or personal property. I am very much obliged to you!

ADOLPH. No, I regard you as his wife. And that's a good deal more than property—for there can be no substitute. TEKLA. Oh, yes! If you only heard that he had married again, all these foolish notions would leave you.—Have you not taken his place with me?

ADOLPH. Well, have I?—And did you ever love him?

TEKLA. Of course, I did!

ADOLPH. And then—

TEKLA. I grew tired of him!

ADOLPH. And if you should tire of me also?

TEKLA. But I won't!

ADOLPH. If somebody else should turn up—one who had all the qualities you are looking for in a man now—suppose only—then you would leave me?

TEKLA. No.

ADOLPH. If he captivated you? So that you couldn't live without him? Then you would leave me, of course?

TEKLA. No, that doesn't follow.

ADOLPH. But you couldn't love two at the same time, could you?

TEKLA. Yes! Why not?

ADOLPH. That's something I cannot understand.

TEKLA. But things exist although you do not understand them. All persons are not made in the same way, you know.

ADOLPH. I begin to see now!

TEKLA. No, really!

ADOLPH. No, really? [A pause follows, during which he seems to struggle with some—memory that will not come back] Do you know, Tekla, that your frankness is beginning to be painful?

TEKLA. And yet it used to be my foremost virtue In your mind, and one that you taught me.

ADOLPH. Yes, but it seems to me as if you were hiding something behind that frankness of yours.

TEKLA. That's the new tactics, you know.

ADOLPH. I don't know why, but this place has suddenly become offensive to me. If you feel like it, we might return home—this evening!

TEKLA. What kind of notion is that? I have barely arrived and I don't feel like starting on another trip.

ADOLPH. But I want to.

TEKLA. Well, what's that to me?—You can go!

ADOLPH. But I demand that you take the next boat with me!

TEKLA. Demand?—What arc you talking about?

ADOLPH. Do you realise that you are my wife?

TEKLA. Do you realise that you are my husband?

ADOLPH. Well, there's a difference between those two things.

TEKLA. Oh, that's the way you are talking now!—You have never loved me!

ADOLPH. Haven't I?

TEKLA. No, for to love is to give.

ADOLPH. To love like a man is to give; to love like a woman is to take.—And I have given, given, given!

TEKLA. Pooh! What have you given?

ADOLPH. Everything!

TEKLA. That's a lot! And if it be true, then I must have taken it. Are you beginning to send in bills for your gifts now? And if I have taken anything, this proves only my love for you. A woman cannot receive anything except from her lover.

ADOLPH. Her lover, yes! There you spoke the truth! I have been your lover, but never your husband.

TEKLA. Well, isn't that much more agreeable—to escape playing chaperon? But if you are not satisfied with your position, I'll send you packing, for I don't want a husband.

ADOLPH. No, that's what I have noticed. For a while ago, when you began to sneak away from me like a thief with his booty, and when you began to seek company of your own where you could flaunt my plumes and display my gems, then I felt, like reminding you of your debt. And at once I became a troublesome creditor whom you wanted to get rid of. You wanted to repudiate your own notes, and in order not to increase your debt to me, you stopped pillaging my safe and began to try those of other people instead. Without having done anything myself, I became to you merely the husband. And now I am going to be your husband whether you like it or not, as I am not allowed to be your lover any longer,

TEKLA. [Playfully] Now he shouldn't talk nonsense, the sweet little idiot!

ADOLPH. Look out: it's dangerous to think everybody an idiot but oneself!

TEKLA. But that's what everybody thinks.

ADOLPH. And I am beginning to suspect that he—your former husband—was not so much of an idiot after all.

TEKLA. Heavens! Are you beginning to sympathise with—him?

ADOLPH. Yes, not far from it,

TEKLA. Well, well! Perhaps you would like to make his acquaintance and pour out your overflowing heart to him? What a striking picture! But I am also beginning to feel drawn to him, as I am growing more and more tired of acting as wetnurse. For he was at least a man, even though he had the fault of being married to me.

ADOLPH. There, you see! But you had better not talk so loud—we might be overheard.

TEKLA. What would it matter if they took us for married people?

ADOLPH. So now you are getting fond of real male men also, and at the same time you have a taste for chaste young men?

TEKLA. There are no limits to what I can like, as you may see. My heart is open to everybody and everything, to the big and the small, the handsome and the ugly, the new and the old—I love the whole world.

ADOLPH. Do you know what that means?

TEKLA. No, I don't know anything at all. I just *feel*.

ADOLPH. It means that old age is near.

TEKLA. There you are again! Take care!

ADOLPH. Take care yourself!

TEKLA. Of what?

ADOLPH. Of the knife!

TEKLA. [Prattling] Little brother had better not play with such dangerous things.

ADOLPH. I have quit playing.

TEKLA. Oh, it's earnest, is it? Dead earnest! Then I'll show you that—you are mistaken. That is to say—you'll never see it, never know it, but all the rest of the world will know It. And you'll suspect it, you'll believe it, and you'll never have another moment's peace. You'll have the feeling of being ridiculous, of being deceived, but you'll never get any proof of it. For that's what married men never get.

ADOLPH. You hate me then?

TEKLA. No, I don't. And I don't think I shall either. But that's probably because you are nothing to me but a child.

ADOLPH. At this moment, yes. But do you remember how it was while the storm swept over us? Then you lay there like an infant in arms and just cried. Then you had to sit on my lap, and I had to kiss your eyes to sleep. Then I had to be your nurse; had to see that you fixed your hair before going out; had to send your shoes to the cobbler, and see that there was food in the house. I had to sit by your side, holding your hand for hours at a time: you were afraid, afraid of the whole world, because you didn't have a single friend, and because you were crushed by the hostility of public opinion. I had to talk courage into you until my mouth was dry and my head ached. I had to make myself believe that I was strong. I had to force myself into believing in the future. And so I brought you back to life, when you seemed already dead. Then you admired me. Then I was the man—not that kind of athlete you had just left, but the man of will-power, the mesmerist who instilled new nervous energy into your flabby muscles and charged your empty brain with a new store of electricity. And then I gave you back your reputation. I brought you new friends, furnished you with a little court of people who, for the sake of friendship to me, let themselves be lured into admiring you. I set you to rule me and my house. Then I painted my best pictures, glimmering with reds and blues on backgrounds of gold, and there was not an exhibition then where I didn't hold a place of honour. Sometimes you were St. Cecilia, and sometimes Mary Stuart—or little Karin, whom King Eric loved. And I turned public attention in your direction. I compelled the clamorous herd to see yon with my own infatuated vision. I plagued them with your personality, forced you literally down their throats, until that sympathy which makes everything possible became yours at last—and you could stand on your own feet. When you reached that far, then my strength was used up, and I collapsed from the overstrain—in lifting you up, I had pushed myself down. I was taken ill, and my illness seemed an annoyance to you at the moment when all life had just begun to smile at you— and sometimes it seemed to me as if, in your heart, there was a secret desire to get rid of your creditor and the witness of your rise. Your love began to change into that of a grown-up sister, and for lack of better I accustomed myself to the new part of little brother. Your tenderness for me remained, and even increased, but it was mingled with a suggestion of pity that had in it a good deal of contempt. And this changed into open scorn as my talent withered and your own sun rose higher. But in some mysterious way the fountainhead of your inspiration seemed to dry up when I could no longer replenish it—or rather when you wanted to show its independence of me. And at last both of us began to lose ground. And then you looked for somebody to put the blame on. A new victim! For you are weak, and you can never carry your own burdens of guilt and debt. And so you picked me for a scapegoat and doomed me to slaughter. But when you cut my thews, you didn't realise that you were also crippling yourself, for by this time our years of common life had made twins of us. You were a shoot sprung from my stem, and you wanted to cut yourself loose before the shoot had put out roots of its own, and that's why you couldn't grow by yourself. And my stem could not spare its main branch—and so stem and branch must die together.

TEKLA. What you mean with all this, of course, is that you have written my books.

ADOLPH. No, that's what you want me to mean in order to make me out a liar. I don't use such crude expressions as you do, and I spoke for something like five minutes to get in all the nuances, all the halftones, all the transitions—but your hand-organ has only a single note in it.

TEKLA. Yes, but the summary of the whole story is that you have written my books.

ADOLPH. No, there is no summary. You cannot reduce a chord into a single note. You cannot translate a varied life into a sum of one figure. I have made no blunt statements like that of having written your books.

TEKLA. But that's what you meant!

ADOLPH. [Beyond himself] I did not mean it.

TEKLA. But the sum of it—

ADOLPH. [Wildly] There can be no sum without an addition. You get an endless decimal fraction for quotient when your division does not work out evenly. I have not added anything.

TEKLA. But I can do the adding myself.

ADOLPH. I believe it, but then I am not doing it.

TEKLA. No. but that's what you wanted to do.

ADOLPH. [Exhausted, closing his eyes] No, no, no—don't speak to me—you'll drive me into convulsions. Keep silent! Leave me alone! You mutilate my brain with your clumsy pincers—you put your claws into my thoughts and tear them to pieces!

(He seems almost unconscious and sits staring straight ahead while his thumbs are bent inward against the palms of his hands.)

TEKLA. [Tenderly] What is it? Are you sick?

(ADOLPH motions her away.)

TEKLA. Adolph!

(ADOLPH shakes his head at her.)

TEKLA. Adolph.

ADOLPH. Yes.

TEKLA. Do you admit that you were unjust a moment ago?

ADOLPH. Yes, yes, yes, yes, I admit!

TEKLA. And do you ask my pardon?

ADOLPH. Yes, yes, yes, I ask your pardon—if you only won't speak to me!

TEKLA. Kiss my hand then!

ADOLPH. [Kissing her hand] I'll kiss your hand—if you only don't speak to me!

TEKLA. And now you had better go out for a breath of fresh air before dinner.

ADOLPH. Yes, I think I need it. And then we'll pack and leave.

TEKLA. No!

ADOLPH. [On his feet] Why? There must be a reason.

TEKLA. The reason is that I have promised to be at the concert to- night.

ADOLPH. Oh, that's it!

TEKLA. Yes, that's it. I have promised to attend—

ADOLPH. Promised? Probably you said only that you might go, and that wouldn't prevent you from saying now that you won't go.

TEKLA. No, I am not like you: I keep my word.

ADOLPH. Of course, promises should be kept, but we don't have to live up to every little word we happen to drop. Perhaps there is somebody who has made you promise to go.

TEKLA. Yes.

ADOLPH. Then you can ask to be released from your promise because your husband is sick.

TEKLA, No, I don't want to do that, and you are not sick enough to be kept from going with me.

ADOLPH. Why do you always want to drag me along? Do you feel safer then?

TEKLA. I don't know what you mean.

ADOLPH. That's what you always say when you know I mean something that—doesn't please you.

TEKLA. So-o! What is it now that doesn't please me?

ADOLPH. Oh, I beg you, don't begin over again—Good-bye for a while!

(Goes out through the door in the rear and then turns to the right.)

(TEKLA is left alone. A moment later GUSTAV enters and goes straight up to the table as if looking for a newspaper. He pretends not to see TEKLA.)

TEKLA. [Shows agitation, but manages to control herself] Oh, is it you?

GUSTAV. Yes, it's me—I beg your pardon!

TEKLA. Which way did you come?

GUSTAV. By land. But—I am not going to stay, as—

TEKLA. Oh, there is no reason why you shouldn't.—Well, it was some time ago—

GUSTAV. Yes, some time.

TEKLA. You have changed a great deal.

GUSTAV. And you are as charming as ever, A little younger, if anything. Excuse me, however—I am not going to spoil your happiness by my presence. And if I had known you were here, I should never—

TEKLA. If you don't think it improper, I should like you to stay.

GUSTAV. On my part there could be no objection, but I fear—well, whatever I say, I am sure to offend you.

TEKLA. Sit down a moment. You don't offend me, for you possess that rare gift—which was always yours—of tact and politeness.

GUSTAV. It's very kind of you. But one could hardly expect—that your husband might regard my qualities in the same generous light as you.

TEKLA. On the contrary, he has just been speaking of you in very sympathetic terms.

GUSTAV. Oh!—Well, everything becomes covered up by time, like names cut in a tree—and not even dislike can maintain itself permanently in our minds.

TEKLA. He has never disliked you, for he has never seen you. And as for me, I have always cherished a dream—that of seeing you come together as friends—or at least of seeing you meet for once in my presence—of seeing you shake hands—and then go your different ways again.

GUSTAV. It has also been my secret longing to see her whom I used to love more than my own life—to make sure that she was in good hands. And although I have heard nothing but good of him, and am familiar with all his work, I should nevertheless have liked, before it grew too late, to look into his eyes and beg him to take good care of the treasure Providence has placed in his possession. In that way I hoped also to lay the hatred that must have developed instinctively between us; I wished to bring some peace and humility into my soul, so that I might manage to live through the rest of my sorrowful days.

TEKLA. You have uttered my own thoughts, and you have understood me. I thank you for it!

GUSTAV. Oh, I am a man of small account, and have always been too insignificant to keep you in the shadow. My monotonous way of living, my drudgery, my narrow horizons—all that could not satisfy a soul like yours, longing for liberty. I admit it. But you understand—you who have searched the human soul—what it cost me to make such a confession to myself.

TEKLA. It is noble, it is splendid, to acknowledge one's own shortcomings—and it's not everybody that's capable of it. [Sighs] But yours has always been an honest, and faithful, and reliable nature—one that I had to respect—but—

GUSTAV. Not always—not at that time! But suffering purifies, sorrow ennobles, and—I have suffered!

TEKLA. Poor Gustav! Can you forgive me? Tell me, can you?

GUSTAV. Forgive? What? I am the one who must ask you to forgive.

TEKLA. [Changing tone] I believe we are crying, both of us—we who are old enough to know better!

GUSTAV. [Feeling his way] Old? Yes, I am old. But you—you grow younger every day.

(He has by that time manoeuvred himself up to the chair on the left and sits down on it, whereupon TEKLA sits down on the sofa.)

TEKLA. Do you think so?

GUSTAV. And then you know how to dress.

TEKLA. I learned that from you. Don't you remember how you figured out what colors would be most becoming to me?

GUSTAV. No.

TEKLA. Yes, don't you remember—hm!—I can even recall how you used to be angry with me whenever I failed to have at least a touch of crimson about my dress.

GUSTAV. No, not angry! I was never angry with you.

TEKLA. Oh, yes, when you wanted to teach me how to think—do you remember? For that was something I couldn't do at all.

GUSTAV. Of course, you could. It's something every human being does. And you have become quite keen at it—at least when you write.

TEKLA. [Unpleasantly impressed; hurrying her words] Well, my dear Gustav, it is pleasant to see you anyhow, and especially in a peaceful way like this.

GUSTAV. Well, I can hardly be called a troublemaker, and you had a pretty peaceful time with me.

TEKLA. Perhaps too much so.

GUSTAV. Oh! But you see, I thought you wanted me that way. It was at least the impression you gave me while we were engaged.

TEKLA. Do you think one really knows what one wants at that time? And then the mammas insist on all kinds of pretensions, of course.

GUSTAV. Well, now you must be having all the excitement you can wish. They say that life among artists is rather swift, and I don't think your husband can be called a sluggard.

TEKLA. You can get too much of a good thing.

GUSTAV. [Trying a new tack] What! I do believe you are still wearing the ear-rings I gave you?

TEKLA. [Embarrassed] Why not? There was never any quarrel between us—and then I thought I might wear them as a token—and a reminder—that we were not enemies. And then, you know, it is impossible to buy this kind of ear-rings any longer. [Takes off one of her ear-rings.]

GUSTAV. Oh, that's all right, but what does your husband say of it?

TEKLA. Why should I mind what he says?

GUSTAV. Don't you mind that?—But you may be doing him an injury. It is likely to make him ridiculous.

TEKLA. [Brusquely, as if speaking to herself almost] He was that before!

GUSTAV. [Rises when he notes her difficulty in putting back the ear-ring] May I help you, perhaps?

TEKLA. Oh—thank you!

GUSTAV. [Pinching her ear] That tiny ear!—Think only if your husband could see us now!

TEKLA. Wouldn't he howl, though!

GUSTAV. Is he jealous also?

TEKLA. Is he? I should say so!

[A noise is heard from the room on the right.]

GUSTAV. Who lives in that room?

TEKLA. I don't know.—But tell me how you are getting along and what you are doing?

GUSTAV. Tell me rather how you are getting along?

(TEKLA is visibly confused, and without realising what she is doing, she takes the cover off the wax figure.)

GUSTAV. Hello! What's that?—Well!—It must be you!

TEKLA. I don't believe so.

GUSTAV. But it is very like you.

TEKLA. [Cynically] Do you think so?

GUSTAV. That reminds me of the story—you know it—"How could your majesty see that?"

TEKLA, [Laughing aloud] You are impossible!—Do you know any new stories?

GUSTAV. No, but you ought to have some.

TEKLA. Oh, I never hear anything funny nowadays.

GUSTAV. Is he modest also?

TEKLA. Oh—well—

GUSTAV. Not an everything?

TEKLA. He isn't well just now.

GUSTAV. Well, why should little brother put his nose into other people's hives?

TEKLA. [Laughing] You crazy thing!

GUSTAV. Poor chap!—Do you remember once when we were just married—we lived in this very room. It was furnished differently in those days. There was a chest of drawers against that wall there—and over there stood the big bed.

TEKLA. Now you stop!

GUSTAV. Look at me!

TEKLA. Well, why shouldn't I?

[They look hard at each other.]

GUSTAV. Do you think a person can ever forget anything that has made a very deep impression on him?

TEKLA. No! And our memories have a tremendous power. Particularly the memories of our youth.

GUSTAV. Do you remember when I first met you? Then you were a pretty little girl: a slate on which parents and governesses had made a few scrawls that I had to wipe out. And then I filled it with inscriptions that suited my own mind, until you believed the slate could hold nothing more. That's the reason, you know, why I shouldn't care to be in your husband's place—well, that's his business! But it's also the reason why I take pleasure in meeting you again. Our thoughts fit together exactly. And as I sit here and chat with you, it seems to me like drinking old wine of my own bottling. Yes, it's my own wine, but it has gained a great deal in flavour! And now, when I am about to marry again, I have purposely picked out a young girl whom I can educate to suit myself. For the woman, you know, is the man's child, and if she is not, he becomes hers, and then the world turns topsy-turvy.

TEKLA. Are you going to marry again?

GUSTAV. Yes, I want to try my luck once more, but this time I am going to make a better start, so that it won't end again with a spill.

TEKLA. Is she good looking?

GUSTAV. Yes, to me. But perhaps I am too old. It's queer—now when chance has brought me together with you again—I am beginning to doubt whether it will be possible to play the game over again.

TEKLA. How do you mean?

GUSTAV. I can feel that my roots stick in your soil, and the old wounds are beginning to break open. You are a dangerous woman, Tekla!

TEKLA. Am I? And my young husband says that I can make no more conquests.

GUSTAV. That means he has ceased to love you.

TEKLA. Well, I can't quite make out what love means to him.

GUSTAV. You have been playing hide and seek so long that at last you cannot find each other at all. Such things do happen. You have had to play the innocent to yourself, until he has lost his courage. There *are* some drawbacks to a change, I tell you—there are drawbacks to it, indeed.

TEKLA. Do you mean to reproach—

GUSTAV. Not at all! Whatever happens is to a certain extent necessary, for if it didn't happen, something else would—but now it did happen, and so it had to happen.

TEKLA. *You* are a man of discernment. And I have never met anybody with whom I liked so much to exchange ideas. You are so utterly free from all morality and preaching, and you ask so little of people, that it is possible to be oneself in your presence. Do you know, I am jealous of your intended wife!

GUSTAV. And do you realise that I am jealous of your husband?

TEKLA. [Rising] And now we must part! Forever!

GUSTAV. Yes, we must part! But not without a farewell—or what do you say?

TEKLA. [Agitated] No!

GUSTAV. [Following after her] Yes!—Let us have a farewell! Let us drown our memories—you know, there are intoxications so deep that when you wake up all memories are gone. [Putting his arm around her waist] You have been dragged down by a diseased spirit, who is infecting you with his own anaemia. I'll breathe new life into you. I'll make your talent blossom again in your autumn days, like a remontant rose. I'll—

(Two LADIES in travelling dress are seen in the doorway leading to the veranda. They look surprised. Then they point at those within, laugh, and disappear.)

TEKLA. [Freeing herself] Who was that?

GUSTAV. [Indifferently] Some tourists.

TEKLA. Leave me alone! I am afraid of you!

GUSTAV. Why?

TEKLA. You take my soul away from me!

GUSTAV. And give you my own in its place! And you have no soul for that matter—it's nothing but a delusion.

TEKLA. You have a way of saying impolite things so that nobody can be angry with you.

GUSTAV. It's because you feel that I hold the first mortgage on you—Tell me now, when—and—where?

TEKLA. No, it wouldn't be right to him. I think he is still in love with me, and I don't want to do any more harm.

GUSTAV. He does not love you! Do you want proofs?

TEKLA, Where can you get them?

GUSTAV. [Picking up the pieces of the photograph from the floor] Here! See for yourself!

TEKLA. Oh, that's an outrage!

GUSTAV. Do you see? Now then, when? And where?

TEKLA. The false-hearted wretch!

GUSTAV. When?

TEKLA. He leaves to-night, with the eight-o'clock boat.

GUSTAV. And then—

TEKLA. At nine! [A noise is heard from the adjoining room] Who can be living in there that makes such a racket?

GUSTAV. Let's see! [Goes over and looks through the keyhole] There's a table that has been upset, and a smashed water caraffe— that's all! I shouldn't wonder if they had left a dog locked up in there.—At nine o'clock then?

TEKLA. All right! And let him answer for it himself.—What a depth of deceit! And he who has always preached about truthfulness, and tried to teach me to tell the truth!—But wait a little—how was it now? He received me with something like hostility—didn't meet me at the landing—and then—and then he made some remark about young men on board the boat, which I pretended not to hear— but how could he know? Wait—and then he began to philosophise about women—and then the spectre of you seemed to be haunting him—and he talked of becoming a sculptor, that being the art of the time—exactly in accordance with your old speculations!

GUSTAV. No, really!

TEKLA. No, really?—Oh, now I understand! Now I begin to see what a hideous creature you are! You have been here before and stabbed him to death! It was you who had been sitting there on the sofa; it was you who made him think himself an epileptic—that he had to live in celibacy; that he ought to rise in rebellion against his wife; yes, it was you!—How long have you been here?

GUSTAV. I have been here a week.

TEKLA. It was you, then, I saw on board the boat?

GUSTAV. It was.

TEKLA. And now you were thinking you could trap me?

GUSTAV. It has been done.

TEKLA. Not yet!

GUSTAV. Yes!

TEKLA. Like a wolf you went after my lamb. You came here with a villainous plan to break up my happiness, and you were carrying it out, when my eyes were opened, and I foiled you.

GUSTAV. Not quite that way, if you please. This is how it happened in reality. Of course, it has been my secret hope that disaster might overtake you. But I felt practically certain that no interference on my part was required. And besides, I have been far too busy to have any time left for intriguing. But when I happened to be moving about a bit, and happened to see you with those young men on board the boat, then I guessed the time had come for me to take a look at the situation. I came here, and your lamb threw itself into the arms of the wolf. I won his affection by some sort of reminiscent impression which I shall not be tactless enough to explain to you. At first he aroused my sympathy, because he seemed to be in the same fix as I was once. But then he happened to touch old wounds—that book, you know, and "the idiot"—and I was seized with a wish to pick him to pieces, and to mix up these so thoroughly that they couldn't be put together again—and I succeeded, thanks to the painstaking way in which you had done the work of preparation. Then I had to deal with you. For you were the spring that had kept the works moving, and you had to be taken apart—and what a buzzing followed!—When I came in here, I didn't know exactly what to say. Like a chess-player, I had laid a number of tentative plans, of course, but my play had to depend on your moves. One thing led to the other, chance lent me a hand, and finally I had you where I wanted you.— Now you are caught!

TEKLA. No!

GUSTAV. Yes, you are! What you least wanted has happened. The world at large, represented by two lady tourists—whom I had not sent for, as I am not an intriguer—the world has seen how you became reconciled to your former husband, and how you sneaked back repentantly into his faithful arms. Isn't that enough?

TEKLA. It ought to be enough for your revenge—But tell me, how can you, who are so enlightened and so right-minded—how is it possible that you, who think whatever happens must happen, and that all our actions are determined in advance—

GUSTAV. [Correcting her] To a certain extent determined.

TEKLA. That's the same thing!

GUSTAV. No!

TEKLA. [Disregarding him] How is it possible that you, who hold me guiltless, as I was driven by my nature and the circumstances into acting as I did—how can you think yourself entitled to revenge—?

GUSTAV. For that very reason—for the reason that my nature and the circumstances drove me into seeking revenge. Isn't that giving both sides a square deal? But do you know why you two had to get the worst of it in this struggle?

(TEKLA looks scornful.)

GUSTAV. And why you were doomed to be fooled? Because I am stronger than you, and wiser also. You have been the idiot—and he! And now you may perceive that a man need not be an idiot because he doesn't write novels or paint pictures. It might be well for you to bear this in mind.

TEKLA. Are you then entirely without feelings?

GUSTAV. Entirely! And for that very reason, you know, I am capable of thinking—in which you have had no experience whatever-and of acting—in which you have just had some slight experience.

TEKLA. And all this merely because I have hurt your vanity?

GUSTAV. Don't call that MERELY! You had better not go around hurting other people's vanity. They have no more sensitive spot than that.

TEKLA. Vindictive wretch—shame on you!

GUSTAV. Dissolute wretch—shame on you!

TEKLA. Oh, that's my character, is it?

GUSTAV. Oh, that's my character, is it?—You ought to learn something about human nature in others before you give your own nature free rein. Otherwise you may get hurt, and then there will be wailing and gnashing of teeth.

TEKLA. You can never forgive:—

GUSTAV. Yes, I have forgiven you!

TEKLA. You!

GUSTAV. Of course! Have I raised a hand against you during all these years? No! And now I came here only to have a look at you, and it was enough to burst your bubble. Have I uttered a single reproach? Have I moralised or preached sermons? No! I played a joke or two on your dear consort, and nothing more was needed to finish him.—But there is no reason why I, the complainant, should be defending myself as I am now—Tekla! Have you nothing at all to reproach yourself with?

TEKLA. Nothing at all! Christians say that our actions are governed by Providence; others call it Fate; in either case, are we not free from all liability?

GUSTAV. In a measure, yes; but there is always a narrow margin left unprotected, and there the liability applies in spite of all. And sooner or later the creditors make their appearance. Guiltless, but accountable! Guiltless in regard to one who is no more; accountable to oneself and one's fellow beings.

TEKLA. So you came here to dun me?

GUSTAV. I came to take back what you had stolen, not what you had received as a gift. You had stolen my honour, and I could recover it only by taking yours. This, I think, was my right—or was it not?

TEKLA. Honour? Hm! And now you feel satisfied?

GUSTAV. Now I feel satisfied. [Rings for a waiter.]

TEKLA. And now you are going home to your fiancee?

GUSTAV. I have no fiancee! Nor am I ever going to have one. I am not going home, for I have no home, and don't want one.

(A WAITER comes in.)

GUSTAV. Get me my bill—I am leaving by the eight o'clock boat.

(THE WAITER bows and goes out.)

TEKLA. Without making up?

GUSTAV. Making up? You use such a lot of words that have lost their—meaning. Why should we make up? Perhaps you want all three of us to live together? You, if anybody, ought to make up by making good what you took away, but this you cannot do. You just took, and what you took you consumed, so that there is nothing left to restore.—Will it satisfy you if I say like this: forgive me that you tore my heart to pieces; forgive me that you disgraced me; forgive me that you made me the laughing-stock of my pupils through every week-day of seven long years; forgive me that I set you free from parental restraints, that I released you from the tyranny of ignorance and superstition, that I set you to rule my house, that I gave you position and friends, that I made a woman out of the child you were before? Forgive me as I forgive you!— Now I have torn up your note! Now you can go and settle your account with the other one!

TEKLA. What have you done with him? I am beginning to suspect—something terrible!

GUSTAV. With him? Do you still love him?

TEKLA. Yes!

GUSTAV. And a moment ago it was me! Was that also true?

TEKLA. It was true.

GUSTAV. Do you know what you are then?

TEKLA. You despise me?

GUSTAV. I pity you. It is a trait—I don't call it a fault—just a trait, which is rendered disadvantageous by its results. Poor Tekla! I don't know—but it seems almost as if I were feeling a certain regret, although I am as free from any guilt—as you! But perhaps it will be useful to you to feel what I felt that time.— Do you know where your husband is?

TEKLA. I think I know now—he is in that room in there! And he has heard everything! And seen everything! And the man who sees his own wraith dies!

(ADOLPH appears in the doorway leading to the veranda. His face is white as a sheet, and there is a bleeding scratch on one cheek. His eyes are staring and void of all expression. His lips are covered with froth.)

GUSTAV. [Shrinking back] No, there he is!—Now you can settle with him and see if he proves as generous as I have been.—Good-bye!

(He goes toward the left, but stops before he reaches the door.)

TEKLA. [Goes to meet ADOLPH with open arms] Adolph!

(ADOLPH leans against the door-jamb and sinks gradually to the floor.)

TEKLA. [Throwing herself upon his prostrate body and caressing him] Adolph! My own child! Are you still alive—oh, speak, speak!— Please forgive your nasty Tekla! Forgive me, forgive me, forgive me!—Little brother must say something, I tell him!—No, good God, he doesn't hear! He is dead! O God in heaven! O my God! Help!

GUSTAV. Why, she really must have loved *him*, too!—Poor creature!

(Curtain.)

PARIAH

INTRODUCTION

BOTH "Creditors" and "Pariah" were written in the winter of 1888- 89 at Holte, near Copenhagen, where Strindberg, assisted by his first wife, was then engaged in starting what he called a "Scandinavian Experimental Theatre." In March, 1889, the two plays were given by students from the University of Copenhagen, and with Mrs. von Essen Strindberg as *Tekla*. A couple of weeks later the performance was repeated across the Sound, in the Swedish city of Malmö, on which occasion the writer of this introduction, then a young actor, assisted in the stage management. One of the actors was Gustav Wied, a Danish playwright and novelist, whose exquisite art since then has won him European fame. In the audience was Ola Hansson, a Swedish novelist and poet who had just published a short story from which Strindberg, according to his own acknowledgment on playbill and title-page, had taken the name and the theme of "Pariah."

Mr. Hansson has printed a number of letters (*Tilskueren*, Copenhagen, July, 1912) written to him by Strindberg about that time, as well as some very informative comments of his own. Concerning the performance of Malmö he writes: "It gave me a very unpleasant sensation. What did it mean? Why had Strindberg turned my simple theme upsidedown so that it became unrecognisable? Not a vestige of the 'theme from Ola Hansson' remained. Yet he had even suggested that he and I act the play together, I not knowing that it was to be a duel between two criminals. And he had at first planned to call it 'Aryan and Pariah'—which meant, of course, that the strong Aryan, Strindberg, was to crush the weak Pariah, Hansson, *coram populo*."

In regard to his own story Mr. Hansson informs us that it dealt with "a man who commits a forgery and then tells about it, doing both in a sort of somnambulistic state whereby everything is left vague and undefined." At that moment "Raskolnikov" was in the air, so to speak. And without wanting in any way to suggest imitation, I feel sure that the groundnote of the story was distinctly Dostoievskian. Strindberg himself had been reading Nietzsche and was—largely under the pressure of a reaction against the popular disapproval of his anti-feministic attitude—being driven more and more into a superman philosophy which reached its climax in the two novels "Chandalah" (1889) and "At the Edge of the Sea" (1890). The Nietzschean note is unmistakable in the two plays contained in the present volume.

But these plays are strongly colored by something else—by something that is neither Hansson-Dostoievski nor Strindberg- Nietzsche. The solution of the problem is found in the letters published by Mr. Hansson. These show that while Strindberg was still planning "Creditors," and before he had begun "Pariah," he had borrowed from Hansson a volume of tales by Edgar Allan Poe. It was his first acquaintance with the work of Poe, though not with American literature—for among his first printed work was a series of translations from American humourists; and not long ago a Swedish critic (Gunnar Castrén in

Samtiden, Christiania, June, 1912) wrote of Strindberg's literary beginnings that "he had learned much from Swedish literature, but probably more from Mark Twain and Dickens."

The impression Poe made on Strindberg was overwhelming. He returns to it in one letter after another. Everything that suits his mood of the moment is "Poesque" or "E. P.-esque." The story that seems to have made the deepest impression of all was "The Gold Bug," though his thought seems to have distilled more useful material out of certain other stories illustrating Poe's theories about mental suggestion. Under the direct influence of these theories, Strindberg, according to his own statements to Hansson, wrote the powerful one-act play "Simoom," and made *Gustav* in "Creditors" actually *call forth* the latent epileptic tendencies in *Adolph*. And on the same authority we must trace the method of: psychological detection practised by *Mr. X.* in "Pariah" directly to "The Gold Bug."

Here we have the reason why Mr. Hansson could find so little of his story in the play. And here we have the origin of a theme which, while not quite new to him, was ever afterward to remain a favourite one with Strindberg: that of a duel between intellect and cunning. It forms the basis of such novels as "Chandalah" and "At the Edge of the Sea," but it recurs in subtler form in works of much later date. To readers of the present day, *Mr. X.*—that striking antithesis of everything a scientist used to stand for in poetry—is much less interesting as a superman *in spe* than as an illustration of what a morally and mentally normal man can do with the tools furnished him by our new understanding of human ways and human motives. And in giving us a play that holds our interest as firmly as the best "love plot" ever devised, although the stage shows us only two men engaged in an intellectual wrestling match, Strindberg took another great step toward ridding the drama of its old, shackling conventions.

The name of this play has sometimes been translated as "The Outcast," whereby it becomes confused with "The Outlaw," a much earlier play on a theme from the old Sagas. I think it better, too, that the Hindu allusion in the Swedish title be not lost, for the best of men may become an outcast, but the baseness of the Pariah is not supposed to spring only from lack of social position.

PARIAH
AN ACT
1889

PERSONS

MR. X., an archaeologist, Middle-aged man.
MR. Y., an American traveller, Middle-aged man.

SCENE

(A simply furnished room in a farmhouse. The door and the windows in the background open on a landscape. In the middle of the room stands a big dining-table, covered at one end by books, writing materials, and antiquities; at the other end, by a microscope, insect cases, and specimen jars full of alchohol.)

(On the left side hangs a bookshelf. Otherwise the furniture is that of a well-to-do farmer.)

(MR. Y. enters in his shirt-sleeves, carrying a butterfly-net and a botany-can. He goes straight up to the bookshelf and takes down a book, which he begins to read on the spot.)

(The landscape outside and the room itself are steeped in sunlight. The ringing of church bells indicates that the morning services are just over. Now and then the cackling of hens is heard from the outside.)

(MR. X. enters, also in his shirt-sleeves.)

(MR. Y. starts violently, puts the book back on the shelf upside-down, and pretends to be looking for another volume.)

MR. X. This heat is horrible. I guess we are going to have a thunderstorm.

MR. Y. What makes you think so?

MR. X. The bells have a kind of dry ring to them, the flies are sticky, and the hens cackle. I meant to go fishing, but I couldn't find any worms. Don't you feel nervous?

MR. Y. [Cautiously] I?—A little.

MR. X. Well, for that matter, you always look as if you were expecting thunderstorms.

MR. Y. [With a start] Do I?

MR. X. Now, you are going away tomorrow, of course, so it is not to be wondered at that you are a little "journey-proud."— Anything new?—Oh, there's the mail! [Picks up some letters from the table] My, I have palpitation of the heart every time I open a letter! Nothing but debts, debts, debts! Have you ever had any debts?

MR. Y. [After some reflection] N-no.

MR. X. Well, then you don't know what it means to receive a lot of overdue bills. [Reads one of the letters] The rent unpaid—the landlord acting nasty—my wife in despair. And here am I sitting waist-high in gold! [He opens an iron-banded box that stands on the table; then both sit down at the table, facing each other] Just look—here I have six thousand crowns' worth of gold which I have dug up in the last fortnight. This bracelet alone would bring me the three hundred and fifty crowns I need. And with all of it I might make a fine career for myself. Then I could get the illustrations made for my treatise at once; I could get my work printed, and—I could travel! Why don't I do it, do you suppose?

MR. Y. I suppose you are afraid to be found out.

MR. X. That, too, perhaps. But don't you think an intelligent fellow like myself might fix matters so that he was never found out? I am alone all the time—with nobody watching me—while I am digging out there in the fields. It wouldn't be strange if I put something in my own pockets now and then.

MR. Y. Yes, but the worst danger lies in disposing of the stuff.

MR. X. Pooh! I'd melt it down, of course—every bit of it—and then I'd turn it into coins—with just as much gold in them as genuine ones, of course—

MR. Y. Of course!

MR. X. Well, you can easily see why. For if I wanted to dabble in counterfeits, then I need not go digging for gold first. [Pause] It is a strange thing anyhow, that if anybody else did what I cannot make myself do, then I'd be willing to acquit him—but I couldn't possibly acquit myself. I might even make a brilliant speech in defence of the thief, proving that this gold was *res nullius*, or nobody's, as it had been deposited at a time when property rights did not yet exist; that even under existing rights it could belong only to the first finder of it, as the ground-owner has never included it in the valuation of his property; and so on.

MR. Y. And probably it would be much easier for you to do this if the—hm!—the thief had not been prompted by actual need, but by a mania for collecting, for instance—or by scientific aspirations— by the ambition to keep a discovery to himself. Don't you think so?

MR. X. You mean that I could not acquit him if actual need had been the motive? Yes, for that's the only motive which the law will not accept in extenuation. That motive makes a plain theft of it.

MR. Y. And this you couldn't excuse?

MR. X. Oh, excuse—no, I guess not, as the law wouldn't. On the other hand, I must admit that it would be hard for me to charge a collector with theft merely because he had appropriated some specimen not yet represented in his own collection.

MR. Y. So that vanity or ambition might excuse what could not be excused by need?

MR. X. And yet need ought to be the more telling excuse—the only one, in fact? But I feel as I have said. And I can no more change this feeling than I can change my own determination not to steal under any circumstances whatever.

MR. Y. And I suppose you count it a great merit that you cannot— hm!—steal?

MR. X. No, my disinclination to steal is just as irresistible as the inclination to do so is irresistible with some people. So it cannot be called a merit. I cannot do it, and the other one cannot refrain!—But you understand, of course, that I am not without a desire to own this gold. Why don't I take it then? Because I cannot! It's an inability—and the lack of something cannot be called a merit. There!

[Closes the box with a slam. Stray clouds have cast their shadows on the landscape and darkened the room now and then. Now it grows quite dark as when a thunderstorm is approaching.]

MR. X. How close the air is! I guess the storm is coming all right.

[MR. Y. gets up and shuts the door and all the windows.]

MR. X. Are you afraid of thunder?

MR. Y. It's just as well to be careful.

(They resume their seats at the table.)

MR. X. You're a curious chap! Here you come dropping down like a bomb a fortnight ago, introducing yourself as a Swedish-American who is collecting flies for a small museum—

MR. Y. Oh, never mind me now!

MR. X. That's what you always say when I grow tired of talking about myself and want to turn my attention to you. Perhaps that was the reason why I took to you as I did—because you let me talk about myself? All at once we seemed like old friends. There were no angles about you against which I could bump myself, no pins that pricked. There was something soft about your whole person, and you overflowed with that tact which only well-educated people know how to show. You never made a noise when you came home late at night or got up early in the morning. You were patient in small things, and you gave in whenever a conflict seemed threatening. In a word, you proved yourself the perfect companion! But you were entirely too compliant not to set me wondering about you in the long run—and you are too timid, too easily frightened. It seems almost as if you were made up of two different personalities. Why, as I sit here looking at your back in the mirror over there—it is as if I were looking at somebody else.

(MR. Y. turns around and stares at the mirror.)

MR. X. No, you cannot get a glimpse of your own back, man!—In front you appear like a fearless sort of fellow, one meeting his fate with bared breast, but from behind—really, I don't want to be impolite, but—you look as if you were carrying a burden, or as if you were crouching to escape a raised stick. And when I look at that red cross your suspenders make on your white shirt—well, it looks to me like some kind of emblem, like a trade-mark on a packing-box—

MR. Y. I feel as if I'd choke—if the storm doesn't break soon—

MR. X. It's coming—don't you worry!—And your neck! It looks as if there ought to be another kind of face on top of it, a face quite different in type from yours. And your ears come so close together behind that sometimes I wonder what race you belong to. [A flash of lightning lights up the room] Why, it looked as if that might have struck the sheriff's house!

MR. Y. [Alarmed] The sheriff's!

MR. X. Oh, it just looked that way. But I don't think we'll get much of this storm. Sit down now and let us have a talk, as you are going away to-morrow. One thing I find strange is that you, with whom I have become so intimate in this short time—that yon are one of those whose image I cannot call up when I am away from them. When you are not here, and I happen to think of you, I always get the vision of another acquaintance—one who does not resemble you, but with whom you have certain traits in common.

MR. Y. Who is he?

MR. X. I don't want to name him, but—I used for several years to take my meals at a certain place, and there, at the side-table where they kept the whiskey and the otter preliminaries, I met a little blond man, with blond, faded eyes. He had a wonderful faculty for making his way through a crowd, without jostling anybody or being jostled himself. And from his customary place down by the door he seemed perfectly able to reach whatever he wanted on a table that stood some six feet away from him. He seemed always happy just to be in company. But when he met anybody he knew, then the joy of it made him roar with laughter, and he would hug and pat the other fellow as if he hadn't seen a human face for years. When anybody stepped on his foot, he smiled as if eager to apologise for being in the way. For two years I watched him and amused myself by guessing at his occupation and character. But I never asked who he was; I didn't want to know, you see, for then all the fun would have been spoiled at once. That man had just your quality of being indefinite. At different times I made him out to be a teacher who had never got his licence, a non-commissioned officer, a druggist, a government clerk, a detective— and like you, he looked as if made out of two pieces, for the front of him never quite fitted the back. One day I happened to read in a newspaper about a big forgery committed by a well-known government official. Then I learned that my indefinite gentleman had been a partner of the forger's brother, and that his name was Strawman. Later on I learned that the aforesaid Strawman used to run a circulating library, but that he was now the police reporter of a big daily. How in the world could I hope to establish a connection between the forgery, the police, and my little man's peculiar manners? It was beyond me; and when I asked a friend whether Strawman had ever been punished for something, my friend couldn't answer either yes or no—he just didn't know! [Pause.]

MR. Y. Well, had he ever been—punished?

MR. X. No, he had not. [Pause.]

MR. Y. And that was the reason, you think, why the police had such an attraction for him, and why he was so afraid of offending people?

MR. X. Exactly!

MR. Y. And did you become acquainted with him afterward?

MR. X. No, I didn't want to. [Pause.]

MR. Y. Would you have been willing to make his acquaintance if he had been—punished?

MR. X. Perfectly!

(MR. Y. rises and walks back and forth several times.)

MR. X. Sit still! Why can't you sit still?

MR. Y. How did you get your liberal view of human conditions? Are you a Christian?

MR. X. Oh, can't you see that I am not?

(MR. Y. makes a face.)

MR. X. The Christians require forgiveness. But I require punishment in order that the balance, or whatever you may call it, be restored. And you, who have served a term, ought to know the difference.

MR. Y. [Stands motionless and stares at MR. X., first with wild, hateful eyes, then with surprise and admiration] How—could—you— know—that?

MR. X. Why, I could see it.

MR. Y. How? How could you see it?

MR. X, Oh, with a little practice. It is an art, like many others. But don't let us talk of it any more. [He looks at his watch, arranges a document on the table, dips a pen in the ink-well, and hands it to MR. Y.] I must be thinking of my tangled affairs. Won't you please witness my signature on this note here? I am going to turn it in to the bank at Malmo tomorrow, when I go to the city with you.

MR. Y. I am not going by way of Malmo.

MR. X. Oh, you are not?

MR. Y. No.

MR. X. But that need not prevent you from witnessing my signature.

MR. Y. N-no!—I never write my name on papers of that kind—

MR. X.—any longer! This is the fifth time you have refused to write your own name. The first time nothing more serious was involved than the receipt for a registered letter. Then I began to watch you. And since then I have noticed that you have a morbid fear of a pen filled with ink. You have not written a single letter since you came here—only a post-card, and that you wrote with a blue pencil. You understand now that I have figured out the exact nature of your slip? Furthermore! This is something like the seventh time you have refused to come with me to Malmo, which place you have not visited at all during all this time. And yet you came the whole way from America merely to have a look at Malmo! And every morning you walk a couple of miles, up to the old mill, just to get a glimpse of the roofs of Malmo in the distance. And when you stand over there at the right-hand window and look out through the third pane from the bottom on the left side, yon can see the spired turrets of the castle and the tall chimney of the county jail.—And now I hope you see that it's your own stupidity rather than my cleverness which has made everything clear to me.

MR. Y. This means that you despise me?

MR. X. Oh, no!

MR. Y. Yes, you do—you cannot but do it!

MR. X. No—here's my hand.

(MR. Y. takes hold of the outstretched hand and kisses it.)

MR. X. [Drawing back his hand] Don't lick hands like a dog!

MR. Y. Pardon me, sir, but you are the first one who has let me touch his hand after learning—

MR. X. And now you call me "sir!"—What scares me about you is that you don't feel exonerated, washed clean, raised to the old level, as good as anybody else, when you have suffered your punishment. Do you care to tell me how it happened? Would you?

MR. Y. [Twisting uneasily] Yes, but you won't believe what I say. But I'll tell you. Then you can see for yourself that I am no ORDINARY criminal. You'll become convinced, I think, that there are errors which, so to speak, are involuntary—[twisting again] which seem to commit themselves—spontaneously—without being willed by oneself, and for which one cannot be held responsible— May I open the door a little now, since the storm seems to have passed over?

MR. X. Suit yourself.

MR. Y. [Opens the door; then he sits down at the table and begins to speak with exaggerated display of feeling, theatrical gestures, and a good deal of false emphasis] Yes, I'll tell you! I was a student in the university at Lund, and I needed to get a loan from a bank. I had no pressing debts, and my father owned some property—not a great deal, of course. However, I had sent the note to the second man of the two who were to act as security, and, contrary to expectations, it came back with a refusal. For a while I was completely stunned by the blow, for it was a very unpleasant surprise—most unpleasant! The note was lying in front of me on the table, and the letter lay beside it. At first my eyes stared hopelessly at those lines that pronounced my doom—that is, not a death-doom, of course, for I could easily find other securities, as many as I wanted—but as I have already said, it was very annoying just the same. And as I was sitting there quite unconscious of any evil intention, my eyes fastened upon the signature of the letter, which would have made my future secure if it had only appeared in the right place. It was an unusually well- written signature—and you know how sometimes one may absent- mindedly scribble a sheet of paper full of meaningless words. I had a pen in my hand—[picks up a penholder from the table] like this. And somehow it just began to run—I don't want to claim that there was anything mystical—anything of a spiritualistic nature back of it—for that kind of thing I don't believe in! It was a wholly unreasoned, mechanical process—my copying of that beautiful autograph over and over again. When all the clean space on the letter was used up, I had learned to reproduce the signature automatically—and then—[throwing away the penholder with a violent gesture] then I forgot all about it. That night I slept long and heavily. And when I woke up, I could feel that I had been dreaming, but I couldn't recall the dream itself. At times it was as if a door had been thrown ajar, and then I seemed to see the writing-table with the note on it as in a distant memory—and when I got out of bed, I was forced up to the table, just as if, after careful deliberation, I had formed an irrevocable decision to sign the name to that fateful paper. All thought of the consequences, of the risk involved, had disappeared— no hesitation remained—it was almost as if I was fulfilling some sacred duty—and so I wrote! [Leaps to his feet] What could it be? Was it some kind of outside influence, a case of mental suggestion, as they call it? But from whom could it come? I was sleeping alone in that room. Could it possibly be my primitive self—the savage to whom the keeping of faith is an unknown thing—

which pushed to the front while my consciousness was asleep— together with the criminal will of that self, and its inability to calculate the results of an action? Tell me, what do you think of it?

MR. X. [As if he had to force the words out of himself] Frankly speaking, your story does not convince me—there are gaps in it, but these may depend on your failure to recall all the details— and I have read something about criminal suggestion—or I think I have, at least—hm! But all that is neither here nor there! You have taken your medicine—and you have had the courage to acknowledge your fault. Now we won't talk of it any more.

MR. Y. Yes, yes, yes, we must talk of it—till I become sure of my innocence.

MR. X. Well, are you not?

MR. Y. No, I am not!

MR. X. That's just what bothers me, I tell you. It's exactly what is bothering me!—Don't you feel fairly sure that every human being hides a skeleton in his closet? Have we not, all of us, stolen and lied as children? Undoubtedly! Well, now there are persons who remain children all their lives, so that they cannot control their unlawful desires. Then comes the opportunity, and there you have your criminal.—But I cannot understand why you don't feel innocent. If the child is not held responsible, why should the criminal be regarded differently? It is the more strange because—well, perhaps I may come to repent it later. [Pause] I, for my part, have killed a man, and I have never suffered any qualms on account of it.

MR. Y. [Very much interested] Have—you?

MR. X, Yes, I, and none else! Perhaps you don't care to shake hands with a murderer?

MR. Y. [Pleasantly] Oh, what nonsense!

MR. X. Yes, but I have not been punished,

ME. Y. [Growing more familiar and taking on a superior tone] So much the better for you!—How did you get out of it?

MR. X. There was nobody to accuse me, no suspicions, no witnesses. This is the way it happened. One Christmas I was invited to hunt with a fellow-student a little way out of Upsala. He sent a besotted old coachman to meet me at the station, and this fellow went to sleep on the box, drove the horses into a fence, and upset the whole *equipage* in a ditch. I am not going to pretend that my life was in danger. It was sheer impatience which made me hit him across the neck with the edge of my hand—you know the way—just to wake him up—and the result was that he never woke up at all, but collapsed then and there.

MR. Y. [Craftily] And did you report it?

MR. X. No, and these were my reasons for not doing so. The man left no family behind him, or anybody else to whom his life could be of the slightest use. He had already outlived his allotted period of vegetation, and his place might just as well be filled by somebody more in need of it. On the other hand, my life was necessary to the happiness of my parents and myself, and perhaps also to the progress of my science. The outcome had once for all cured me of any desire to wake up people in that manner, and I didn't care to spoil both my own life and that of my parents for the sake of an abstract principle of justice.

MR. Y. Oh, that's the way you measure the value of a human life?

MR. X. In the present case, yes.

MR. Y. But the sense of guilt—that balance you were speaking of?

MR. X. I had no sense of guilt, as I had committed no crime. As a boy I had given and taken more than one blow of the same kind, and the fatal outcome in this particular case was simply caused by my ignorance of the effect such a blow might have on an elderly person.

MR. Y. Yes, but even the unintentional killing of a man is punished with a two-year term at hard labour—which is exactly what one gets for—writing names.

MR. X. Oh, you may be sure I have thought of it. And more than one night I have dreamt myself in prison. Tell me now—is it really as bad as they say to find oneself behind bolt and bar?

MR. Y. You bet it is!—First of all they disfigure you by cutting off your hair, and if you don't look like a criminal before, you are sure to do so afterward. And when you catch sight of yourself in a mirror you feel quite sure that you are a regular bandit.

MR. X. Isn't it a mask that is being torn off, perhaps? Which wouldn't be a bad idea, I should say.

MR. Y. Yes, you can have your little jest about it!—And then they cut down your food, so that every day and every hour you become conscious of the border line between life and death. Every vital function is more or less checked. You can feel yourself shrinking. And your soul, which was to be cured and improved, is instead put on a starvation diet—pushed back a thousand years into outlived ages. You are not permitted to read anything but what was written for the savages who took part in the migration of the peoples. You hear of nothing but what will never happen in heaven; and what actually does happen on the earth is kept hidden from you. You are torn out of your surroundings, reduced from your own class, put beneath those who are really beneath yourself. Then you get a sense of living in the bronze age. You come to feel as if you were dressed in skins, as if you were living in a cave and eating out of a trough—ugh!

MR. X. But there is reason back of all that. One who acts as if he belonged to the bronze age might surely be expected to don the proper costume.

MR. Y. [Irately] Yes, you sneer! You who have behaved like a man from the stone age—and who are permitted to live in the golden age.

MR. X. [Sharply, watching him closely] What do you mean with that last expression—the golden age?

MR. Y. [With a poorly suppressed snarl] Nothing at all.

MR. X. Now you lie—because you are too much of a coward to say all you think.

MR. Y. Am I a coward? You think so? But I was no coward when I dared to show myself around here, where I had had to suffer as I did.—But can you tell what makes one suffer most while in there?— It is that the others are not in there too!

MR. X. What others?

MR. Y. Those that go unpunished.

MR. X. Are you thinking of me?

MR. Y. I am.

MR. X. But I have committed no crime.

MR. Y. Oh, haven't you?

MR. X. No, a misfortune is no crime.

MR. Y. So, it's a misfortune to commit murder?

MR. X. I have not committed murder.

MR. Y. Is it not murder to kill a person?

MR. X. Not always. The law speaks of murder, manslaughter, killing in self-defence—and it makes a distinction between intentional and unintentional killing. However—now you really frighten me, for it's becoming plain to me that you belong to the most dangerous of all human groups—that of the stupid.

MR. Y. So you imagine that I am stupid? Well, listen—would you like me to show you how clever I am?

MR. X. Come on!

MR. Y. I think you'll have to admit that there is both logic and wisdom in the argument I'm now going to give you. You have suffered a misfortune which might have brought you two years at hard labor. You have completely escaped the disgrace of being punished. And here you see before you a man—who has also suffered a misfortune—the victim of an unconscious impulse—and who has had to stand two years of hard labor for it. Only by some great scientific achievement can this man wipe off the taint that has become attached to him without any fault of his own—but in order to arrive at some such achievement, he must have money—a lot of money—and money this minute! Don't you think that the other one, the unpunished one, would bring a little better balance into these unequal human conditions if he paid a penalty in the form of a fine? Don't you think so?

MR. X. [Calmly] Yes.

MR. Y. Then we understand each other.—Hm! [Pause] What do you think would be reasonable?

MR. X. Reasonable? The minimum fine in such a case is fixed by the law at fifty crowns. But this whole question is settled by the fact that the dead man left no relatives.

MR. Y. Apparently you don't want to understand. Then I'll have to speak plainly: it is to me you must pay that fine.

MR. X. I have never heard that forgers have the right to collect fines imposed for manslaughter. And, besides, there is no prosecutor.

MR. Y. There isn't? Well—how would I do?

MR. X. Oh, *now* we are getting the matter cleared up! How much do you want for becoming my accomplice?

MR. Y. Six thousand crowns.

MR. X. That's too much. And where am I to get them?

(MR. Y. points to the box.)

MR. X. No, I don't want to do that. I don't want to become a thief.

MR. Y. Oh, don't put on any airs now! Do you think I'll believe that you haven't helped yourself out of that box before?

MR. X. [As if speaking to himself] Think only, that I could let myself be fooled so completely. But that's the way with these soft natures. You like them, and then it's so easy to believe that they like you. And that's the reason why I have always been on my guard against people I take a liking to!—So you are firmly convinced that I have helped myself out of the box before?

MR. Y. Certainly! MR. X. And you are going to report me if you don't get six thousand crowns?

MR. Y. Most decidedly! You can't get out of it, so there's no use trying.

MR. X. You think I am going to give my father a thief for son, my wife a thief for husband, my children a thief for father, my fellow-workers a thief for colleague? No, that will never happen!— Now I am going over to the sheriff to report the killing myself.

MR. Y. [Jumps up and begins to pick up his things] Wait a moment!

MR. X. For what?

MR. Y. [Stammering] Oh, I thought—as I am no longer needed—it wouldn't be necessary for me to stay—and I might just as well leave.

MR. X. No, you may not!—Sit down there at the table, where you sat before, and we'll have another talk before you go.

MR. Y. [Sits down after having put on a dark coat] What are you up to now?

MR. X. [Looking into the mirror back of MR. Y.] Oh, now I have it! Oh-h-h!

MR. Y. [Alarmed] What kind of wonderful things are you discovering now?

MR. X. I see in the mirror that you are a thief—a plain, ordinary thief! A moment ago, while you had only the white shirt on, I could notice that there was something wrong about my book-shelf. I couldn't make out just what it was, for I had to listen to you and watch you. But as my antipathy increased, my vision became more acute. And now, with your black coat to furnish the needed color contrast For the red back of the book, which before couldn't be seen against the red of your suspenders—now I see that you have been reading about forgeries in Bernheim's work on mental suggestion—for you turned the book upside-down in putting it back. So even that story of yours was stolen! For tins reason I think myself entitled to conclude that your crime must have been prompted by need, or by mere love of pleasure.

MR. Y. By need! If you only knew—

MR. X. If *you* only knew the extent of the need I have had to face and live through! But that's another story! Let's proceed with your case. That you have been in prison—I take that for granted. But it happened in America, for it was American prison life you described. Another thing may also be taken for granted, namely, that you have not borne your punishment on this side.

MR. Y. How can you imagine anything of the kind?

MR. X. Wait until the sheriff gets here, and you'll learn all about it.

(MR. Y. gets up.)

ME. X. There you see! The first time I mentioned the sheriff, in connection with the storm, you wanted also to run away. And when a person has served out his time he doesn't care to visit an old mill every day just to look at a prison, or to stand by the window—in a word, you are at once punished and unpunished. And that's why it was so hard to make you out. [Pause.]

MR. Y. [Completely beaten] May I go now?

MR. X. Now you can go.

MR. Y. [Putting his things together] Are you angry at me?

MR. X. Yes—would you prefer me to pity you?

MR. Y. [Sulkily] Pity? Do you think you're any better than I?

MR. X. Of course I do, as I AM better than you. I am wiser, and I am less of a menace to prevailing property rights.

MR. Y. You think you are clever, but perhaps I am as clever as you. For the moment you have me checked, but in the next move I can mate you—all the same!

MR. X. [Looking hard at MR. Y.] So we have to have another bout! What kind of mischief are you up to now?

MR. Y. That's my secret.

MR. X. Just look at me—oh, you mean to write my wife an anonymous letter giving away MY secret!

MR. Y. Well, how are you going to prevent it? You don't dare to have me arrested. So you'll have to let me go. And when I am gone, I can do what I please.

MR. X. You devil! So you have found my vulnerable spot! Do you want to make a real murderer out of me?

MR. Y. That's more than you'll ever become—coward!

MR. X. There you see how different people are. You have a feeling that I cannot become guilty of the same kind of acts as you. And that gives you the upper hand. But suppose you forced me to treat you as I treated that coachman?

[He lifts his hand as if ready to hit MR. Y.]

MR. Y. [Staring MR. X. straight in the face] You can't! It's too much for one who couldn't save himself by means of the box over there.

ME. X. So you don't think I have taken anything out of the box?

MR. Y. You were too cowardly—just as you were too cowardly to tell your wife that she had married a murderer.

MR. X. You are a different man from what I took you to be—if stronger or weaker, I cannot tell—if more criminal or less, that's none of my concern—but decidedly more stupid; that much is quite plain. For stupid you were when you wrote another person's name instead of begging—as I have had to do. Stupid you were when you stole things out of my book—could you not guess that I might have read my own books? Stupid you were when you thought yourself cleverer than me, and when you thought that I could be lured into becoming a thief. Stupid you were when you thought balance could be restored by giving the world two thieves instead of one. But most stupid of all you were when you thought I had failed to provide a safe corner-stone for my happiness. Go ahead and write my wife as many anonymous letters as you please about her husband having killed a man—she knew that long before we were married!— Have you had enough now?

MR. Y. May I go?

MR. X. Now you *have* to go! And at once! I'll send your things after you!— Get out of here!

(Curtain.)

Echo Library
www.echo-library.com

Echo Library uses advanced digital print-on-demand technology to build and preserve an exciting world class collection of rare and out-of-print books, making them readily available for everyone to enjoy.

Situated just yards from Teddington Lock on the River Thames, Echo Library was founded in 2005 by Tom Cherrington, a specialist dealer in rare and antiquarian books with a passion for literature.

Please visit our website for a complete catalogue of our books, which includes foreign language titles.

The Right to Read

Echo Library actively supports the Royal National Institute for the Blind's Right to Read initiative by publishing a comprehensive range of Large Print (16 point Tiresias font as recommended by the RNIB) and Clear Print (13 point Tiresias font) titles for those who find standard print difficult to read.

Customer Service

If there is a serious error in the text or layout please send details to feedback@echo-library.com and we will supply a corrected copy. If there is a printing fault or the book is damaged please refer to your supplier.

2-10
do
coll. dev.

LaVergne, TN USA
05 January 2010

168858LV00005B/220/A